THE MURPHY

THE MURPHY

SPIKE MILLIGAN

First published in Great Britain in 2000 by
Virgin Publishing Ltd
Thames Wharf Studios
Rainville Road
London W6 9HA

A catalogue record for this book is available from the British
Library.

ISBN 1 85227 869 2

Typeset by TW Typesetting, Plymouth, Devon.

Printed and bound in Great Britain by CPD, Wales.

Contents

Chapter 1

The spring on the rusting bed creaked as Murphy arose. He used the spring as an alarm clock. Wavering, he sat on the edge of the bed.

'Jesus, why was I born so poor?'

The answer was, because he had no money.

'Dat's it, I've no bloody money, dat's why I'm poor.' He went to put his braces on and mimed, 'I'll get it right one day, you'll see.'

He held a Guinness bottle to the light. It was empty.

'Ah, dat's because it's all in me!'

He was due at the building site at 7.30.

'Seven-tirty,' he groaned. 'What a terrible time to start laying bricks.'

He was trying hard to imagine what the time was. It could be anything. Outside it was daylight, so the night must have gone. He guessed it was six-thirty, then quarter past nine, then two minutes past eleven or midday. He dismissed them all and settled on six-thirty. He felt that it was six-thirty but then, it could be quarter past nine, two minutes past eleven or midday.

He pulled one trouser leg on. I better do the other one, too, he thought.

None of this was easy with his braces already in place, but nothing had ever come easily to Murphy.

On the bus to the site, he met his old mate, Docherty.

'Oh, fancy meetin' you here,' said Murphy.

'Yes, here is where I am,' agreed Docherty.

'Do you see much of Gillen Yates?' Murphy asked.

'No, not much,' said Docherty. 'She's always wearing clothes.'

'Jesus, she's terrible pretty,' said Murphy.

'That she is,' agreed Docherty.

'I see her at Mass every Sunday,' said Murphy.

'So dat's why you go,' giggled Docherty.

The bus arrived at the site. It was raining.

'Feck dis,' said Murphy, as he sat down in the workmen's tin hut.

'You're late, Murphy,' said the foreman, Sean Dillon, from a tin hat.

'For Christ's sake,' said Murphy, scowling round at the teeming rain, 'who wants to be early for dis?'

Dillon couldn't think of *anybody* who would want to be early for dis, certainly nobody in Sligo. The rain in Sligo was like smallpox in Calcutta: it just wouldn't stop. Murphy poured himself a cup of tea.

'Jesus, this tea is piss poor,' he groaned.

'Yes, 'tis the speciality of dis house,' said Dillon. 'Now, listen, Murphy. Der company is willin' ter pay tree pence extra per hour if you'll work in der rain.'

'*Tree* pence an hour,' moaned Murphy. 'Supposin' I get der pneumonia.'

'You'll earn an extra tree pence an hour for gettin' it,' said Dillon, pouring himself a cup of piss-poor tea.

'Ah, God, does it never stop rainin' in Sligo?' asked Murphy, sipping piss-poor tea.

'Yes. I remember,' said Dillon. 'It was a Tuesday last month.'

THE MURPHY

'What was it like?' Murphy asked.

'Very nice,' said Dillon, rolling a cigarette.

'How many of dem do you smoke?' Murphy asked.

'You know, I can't remember,' Dillon admitted.

'Oh, dey must be doin' somethin' terrible to you if youse can't remember,' said Murphy. 'Dere must be somethin' terrible wrong wid youse.'

'Oh, yes, dere must be somethin' terrible wrong wid me right enough,' Dillon agreed. 'But I can't remember what it is.' The rolled cigarette disintegrated in his hand. 'Oh, feck,' he said.

'Yes, oh, feck,' said Murphy, sympathising. 'I tink,' he continued, 'oi'll go fer dat tree pence an hour extra fer workin' in der rain.'

He rose, walked to the brick pile and started working at tree pence an hour extra in the rain. Three hours later he returned to the hut.

'Der company owes me twelve pence,' he announced.

'Nine,' said Dillon.

So Murphy went out and worked another hour.

Dat must be twelve now, he thought.

He spent the rest of the day in the tin hut.

'Jesus,' he said. ''Tis a terrible life.'

'Yes, I never figured how it got to be dis way,' agreed Dillon.

That evening Murphy drew his wages: three pounds and four shillings. He proceeded to spend it all at The King's. He paid for everyone, especially himself. He would be glad when he'd had enough, and that was just an hour after entering.

'Jesus, was dere ever a better drink?' he said, swallowing pint after pint of Guinness.

'I tink you've had enough,' said the barman to a figure lying flat on the floor.

'He's goin' to feel dis in der mornin',' said a man lying flat on the floor next to him.

The bed spring awoke Murphy at midday.

'Jesus, I've overslept. Oh, my bloody head!'

'Get out of bed, you lazy bugger!' Molly, his wife – yes, suddenly he remembered he had a wife called Molly – screeched at him, bringing a frying pan down on his head.

'Stop dat!' he shouted.

But she didn't stop dat, bringing the pan down on his head again.

'Youse will pay fer dis,' he howled.

'No, I won't,' said Molly. 'I'm doin' it fer free!' And she hit him again fer free.

'Can I have some breakfast, please?' he grovelled.

'Breakfast!' she shouted. 'It's bloody midday!'

'How about some lunch, den?' he suggested.

Molly threw some food at him.

'Dis is der worst lunch I ever had,' he said, chewing on last night's cold chips. 'Can't you warm dem up?' he whined.

'No, dey do dat once dey are inside you,' was the reply.

Why in god's name had he married her? She wasn't pretty; she was fat. And on top of that she was a terrible feck.

'Youse will lose a morning's pay, you lazy bastard. Do you hear me?' she screamed.

'Oh, yes, I can hear you,' he said. In fact, people three streets away could hear her. 'Oh, Molly, I know I've been a bad husband to you . . .'

'*You* know?' she yelled. 'Everybody in Sligo knows it!'

'Molly, darlin', I'll make it up ter you.'

'It's too late fer dat. But fer us being Catholics, I'd have divorced you bloody years ago.' Divorced? Nivver! She'd have to get der Pope to agree ter dat.

'Fer God's sake when will youse stop bloody rowing?' It was Silé, his lovely eighteen-year-old daughter.

'We've stopped now, darlin',' he promised.

The frying pan blows had affected his mind, a very small target.

'Who am I?' he asked, lying helpless on the bed.

'Well, if you don't know, I'm not going to tell youse,' said Molly.

Actually, Molly wasn't really sure who he was. He deserved that. It was bad enough being Irish without this.

As he drifted in and out of a frying pan-induced stupor, Murphy desperately grasped at familiar memories. Who was he? His mind spun like a roulette wheel and the first slot into which his clattering focus settled housed memories of his parents . . .

Family

Chapter 2

Murphy hadn't seen his parents for 30 years. They lived in Buncrana, in Donegal – that was two hundred miles away, that's why he hadn't seen them. It was hard to see from that distance. If they lived closer, he would be able to see them.

He took the train to Buncrana, buying a third class ticket. 'No, I don't want a return,' he said. 'I'll make my own way back.'

From the station at Buncrana, he walked to his parents' house. It was midday when he arrived at the cottage door, just in time for lunch. He knocked on the door and the knocker fell off, so he shouted through the letter box.

'Mum! Dad! It's me, Michael, your son!'

His father opened the door, a look of horror on his face.

'Mick! Mick! We tort you was dead!' said his father. 'We bin laying flowers on a grave for der last five years.'

'I'm sorry I'm such a disappointment to you,' apologised Murphy.

'What are youse doin' down dere?' asked his father.

'I was shoutin' tru der letterbox.'

'Well, what do you want?'

'I come to see you and Mudder.'

'Is dat why . . .' nodded his father.

'Yes,' said Murphy. 'I tort you would be pleased to see me.' He stood waiting. 'Can I come in?'

'Oh, you want to come in?' asked his father, and yanked the door open as far as its creaking hinges would allow.

The front door opened into a single room lit by a crackling peat fire over which hung a large kettle. Seated by the fire was an old woman.

'Mudder, my mudder!' cried Murphy.

'I'm not yer mudder,' said the woman. 'I'm yer Aunty Rose. Yer mudder is in der kitchen, plucking a chicken.'

'Who's dat?' said Mudder, entering the room. There stood her long-lost son. 'Oh, Michael, my son,' she sobbed, embracing him. 'We tort you was dead. Every Sunday we have a Mass said for the dear departed. Why, oh, why didn't you write?'

'I can't write,' he admitted.

'Dat's no excuse,' said his father. 'Youse could have typed it.'

'We've just finished lunch, Son,' said his mudder. Feck. 'Come, sit by the fire.'

Aunty Rose was ushered out of the way to give pride of place at the fireside to the homecoming son.

'Will you be staying long, Son?' his father asked.

'Until the money runs out,' said Murphy.

'Your money?' asked his father.

'No, yours,' said Murphy. 'You see, I'm skint.'

'So den, how long do you tink you'll stay?' asked his father.

'Until you're skint,' said Murphy.

'Den you'd better be going,' said his father. 'We're skint, too.'

'Can't you sell something?' asked Murphy.

12

'We haven't got anything to sell!' said his father.

'What about the piano?' asked Murphy.

'What about the piano?'

'Dat should fetch a good price.'

'Dat was our wedding present!'

'Well, sell it to somebody else as a wedding present.'

'My uncle would kill me.'

'Not till after you sold it.'

'You're not talking like a son of mine!'

'Whose son am I talking like?'

'Have you come here to torture me and yer mudder?'

'Of course not. If I had, I would have brought the branding irons.'

'I don't tink dat's funny.'

'So, dat's why you're not laughing.'

'My son, my son,' said his mudder. 'Don't stand dere arguing wid yer father. He's not up to it since his sterilisation operation. Sit down and have a cup of tea.'

'Haven't you anything stronger, Mudder?' he asked. He hadn't come two hundred bloody miles to drink tea.

'Oh, yes, we have some Worcester sauce.'

'Feck it.'

'Oh, my son, you mustn't say dat. If der Pope heard you say dat he would excommunicate youse.'

'He's too far away to have heard it. Have you no Jameson's, Mudder?'

'Oh, yes, but we only drink it after a funeral.'

'All right, I'll wait fer one.'

'You'll have to be patient, son,' warned his mudder. 'Not many people die around here.'

'Why, what's wrong wid dem?'

'Dere's nuffin' wrong wid dem. Dat's why dey're not dying.'

Just my bloody luck, thought Murphy. 'Can we not try a drap of der whisky, Father?' he asked.

'A drap of der . . .' muttered his father. Unlocking a cupboard, he drew out a bottle and poured.

Murphy tossed it back and held out the glass.

'No,' said his father, taking the glass. He filled it to the brim, tilted his head to throw the drink down his throat, missed and threw it over his shoulder. 'Oh dear, oh dear,' he mumbled. He placed the bottle back in the cupboard, locked it and swallowed the key.

'Look, I only want one more little sip,' pleaded Murphy, reaching behind and retrieving the bottle through the non-existent back of the cupboard. It had been destroyed many years ago when his father had packed the whole family inside it in an attempt to take them all to Dublin by train at freight rates.

'All right, Mick,' said his mudder. 'Just a little sip. Leave enough for der funeral.'

Murphy drank a little sip after a little sip and, not to be outdone, his father did likewise, leaving a little sip for the funeral. Jesus, dat felt better. Why did people have to have bloody funerals? Because they were dead, dat's why. One day he'd have a funeral, but he wouldn't know dat, he'd be in der box.

'What are you tinkin' of, Son?' asked his father.

'I was tinkin' of me funeral.'

'When is dat?'

'I don't know yet. I was only tinkin' of it.'

'Can't you tink of anything else?'

'Yes, I can tink of Ghandi.'

'What bloody good is that?' His father frowned. 'He's an Indian.'

'Yes, dere's millions of dem.'

'It's dere own fault.'

'Yes, dey can't stop fecking.'

'Oh, Son,' his mudder objected. 'Dat word.'

'Yes, but fecking is what causes dem.'

'Is dat so . . .?' said his father. 'Fecking . . . we live and learn.'

'I'll show dem,' Murphy muttered.

'What are youse goin' ter show dem?' asked his father.

'I'm not quite sure at der moment,' Murphy confessed, 'but when I am, then I'll show dem it.'

Murphy's father drained the last of the Jameson's. 'Feck der funeral,' he said.

'Why didn't you let me do dat, Dad?' Murphy complained.

'Because I did it,' his father explained.

'You should be ashamed of yourself,' said Mudder.

'Oh, I am, I am,' said Murphy's father, the bloody liar.

Never mind dat. All would be forgiven by confession. Yes, der Catluck religion was der finest in the world if you kept practising it. If you didn't, you'd soon be left behind with the Protestants. Murphy's old sergeant in the army, Sam Paisley, was one of them. He was a real bastard – and Scottish. Someone should steal up under his kilt and set fire to his balls.

St Patrick was a good Catholic. He drove all the snakes from Ireland; he must have had a big van. Why he wasn't bitten to death, Murphy could never fathom. Maybe it was the drink made the poison useless. Was Ireland cursed with the drink? Murphy didn't know what percentage of the Irish was alcoholic, but it was well over a hundred percent of him.

Yes, St Patrick drove all the snakes from Ireland, even from Belfast. Belfast – that must be the worst city in the world apart from Calcutta. They didn't kill each other in Calcutta, they just died from the smells.

All of these pearls of wisdom, Murphy shared with his parents at the fireside in a long, meandering, whisky-inspired, drivelling ramble.

Yes, the only people safe in Belfast were the Jews. They were lucky – they only died from heart attacks or eating pork. Strange people the Jews. They got lost in the desert and, on top of that, when they were born, they chopped a bit off their willy. Murphy reckoned that's why their women were never satisfied. Their leader, Moses, he got the Ten Commandments.

'So he's der bastard who's made life hell for der Irish trying to keep dem!' said his father.

'Yes,' said Murphy, 'and when dey left der desert, dey all became solicitors, and der failures became bookmakers.'

'Dey've got a lot of my bloody money,' said his father.

'What do you mean a lot?'

'He means dey got the bloody lot. Dey got it all,' said Mudder, spitting in the fire and putting it out. 'I'll soon get it going again.' She took a mouthful of methylated spirits, spat it into the fire and it flared up.

'Yes, I suppose dat is one way,' said Murphy. 'Dat must taste terrible.'

'No, dey say its der favourite drink in Australia.'

Despite Mudder's efforts, the peat fire was running low.

'Mick, would youse like to dig some more?' asked his father, handing Murphy a peat cutting tool.

Christ! Had he come 200 miles to dig bloody peat? Yes, he *had*. Feck. After a few minutes digging, he carried the bag back indoors.

'Tank you, my son,' said Mudder. 'Your father is too old to cut peat any more. If you hadn't come, we would have had to light der oil stove.'

The giant kettle boiled and they made tea. Irish tea. It looked like the Black Death.

'Could I have some milk, Mudder?' Murphy asked.

'Yes, dere's a cow outside.'

'Oh, God,' he said, milking the cow. It squirted all over his trousers and, when it dried, his trousers set hard. He couldn't bend his legs, so he had to walk stiff-legged like a robot.

'Now, dear boy, what have you been doin' all dese years?' asked Mudder, as Murphy goose-stepped back into the cottage.

Mostly, he'd been doing Molly. 'Well, I bin doin' dis and dat,' he said.

'Jesus,' said his father. 'What is dis and dat?'

'Der dises, I was a laundry box washer of der shitty sheets from Sligo General Hospital. Der dats, I worked in a funeral parlour sellin' coffins.'

'Was dat a good job, son?' asked Mudder.

'Oh, yes. People kept dying, especially in der bronchitis season. We had to order extra coffins and stockpile dem.'

'Oh, I'm so proud of you, my son,' said Mudder.

'How long are you stayin'?' said his father. 'We've only der one bed.'

'Oh, don't worry, Dad. I can sleep on der floor,' said Murphy.

'No, yer farder can sleep on der floor and you'll sleep in der bed,' Mudder insisted.

'Feck,' said his father.

'You look hungry, Son,' said Mudder.

17

That's because he was. If he went on any longer, he would faint. Mudder frustrated this with a jam sandwich. He hated jam. You never knew where it had been. In a jar, yes, but then where after that? It could get into all sorts of places.

Murphy remembered he had broken his arm in two places.

'Den youse shouldn't go to dose places,' said his father.

The afternoon wore on and Murphy wore out after fifty games of draughts, thirty cups of tea and eighteen jam sandwiches. As expected, the jam got into all sorts of places. Jam got everywhere: on his fingers, on his nose, even on the dog. When he barked the jam spread to his tail.

'Waste not, want not,' said Mudder, scraping the jam from the tail and back into the pot.

'Dat's very unhygienic,' said his father. 'You might catch something from a dog's tail, it's directly above his arsehole.'

'Oh, I was careful not to touch his arsehole,' said Mudder.

'It would be terrible to catch rabies,' said his father.

'Rabies is at der udder end to his arsehole,' said Mudder, and sighed. 'Tree weeks to Christmas.'

'Christmas!' growled his father. 'I'm only just gettin' over der last one. I still haven't worn the socks you bought me.'

'Why not?'

'Dey are too bloody small, dat's why,' he said.

'You drank der bloody whisky,' said Mudder.

'Ah, dat's because it was der right size,' said his father.

'Are youse keepin' up goin' to Mass?' his Mudder asked Murphy.

'Oh, no, I've given up all dat blarney,' said Murphy, easing his jockstrap.

18

'My son, dat's a mortal sin.'

'Is dat wot it is?' said Murphy, still trying to adjust his jockstrap.

'Stop playin' wid yerself, man,' said his father.

'Yes,' said Mudder. 'Mortal sin.'

'No, Mudder, 'tis not a mortal sin fer playin wid yerself.'

'It *is* fer missin' Mass,' she replied. 'When you die, you'll burn in hell fire for all eternity.'

Eternity? Surely he wouldn't be dead *that* long? Anyhow, how do they get enough coal to keep it going? No, Hell was a lot of bollocks. Being Catholic was hell. If you committed a sin you had to confess it.

He remembered his first confession. He told the priest, 'I squeezed a woman's boobs.'

'What are boobs?' asked the young priest.

'Dem's part of her chest,' Murphy explained.

'Ah, you mean tits!' said the priest.

Oh, those carefree teenaged days.

'What do you do to occupy yerself all day, Mudder?' Murphy asked.

'Well, I start der mornings saying a prayer to der Virgined Mary. Den I has a wash, den I cooks breakfast, den I reads der *Irish Times*. Den I says a prayer to der Virgined Mary, den I wake der bugger up. Dat takes a good hour, der bugger. Den I go shoppin', den I makes a cup of tea and puts me feet up.'

'Put dem up where?' said Murphy.

'Sometimes on a stick, sometimes on der dog.'

'Oh, you do have a busy day,' said Murphy.

'And I has a busy night wid yer father at me nonstop,' added Mudder.

Murphy had had enough. Despite the offer of sleeping in the bed, he decided to set off for home.

'Well, Mudder, I must be going,' he said, putting on his father's overcoat. 'I've got an appointment wid der street.'

Walking straight-legged all the way to Sligo, with his trousers stiff with stale milk, was hell: he slept by night in barns along the way, so each morning he had to get the farm hands to stand him up and get him going. One rainy night he eventually arrived home in Sligo.

'God, man, where have youse been? You've been away fer days!' said Molly. 'And dat's not your overcoat.'

'No, it's my father's.'

'And what's dat sick all down der front?'

'Oh, dat's mine.'

'What are you doin' in yer father's overcoat?'

'Tryin' ter keep warm.'

'Yer legs,' said Molly. 'What's wrong wid yer legs?'

'I must change me trousers, Molly.'

'Why? What have you done in them?'

'I haven't done anytin' in dem but walk,' he protested.

Thanks to shorts, he was finally able to bend his legs once more, although this would ultimately have a drastic effect on his health. Yes, health was yet another facet of life with which Murphy had never had much luck . . .

Health

Chapter 3

It was Murphy's appointment with the dentist where his shorts started his decline in health. He had to sit in the waiting room wearing the bloody things.

A man sitting opposite him said, 'Sir, your balls are exposed.'

So Murphy crossed his legs and crushed them. The pain made him faint.

'What happened?' he said, when he came to.

'You crushed your balls,' said the man. The thought of it immediately made Murphy faint again.

When the dentist called his name, Murphy entered the surgery and the dental nurse screamed. She had never seen a Sligo man in shorts before, nor fat, hairy legs.

'Look,' said the dentist, 'could you come back again in trousers?'

Feck.

Back out on the street, Murphy had nothing to do, so he walked. Eventually, after a mile or so, that became boring, so he started to run. That soon buggered him up. Feck. To alleviate the boredom, he started to whistle. As he passed a window, it shot open and a man leaned out screaming, 'Stop dat whistling, dere's people in here trying to sleep.'

But the urge to whistle was upon him, so Murphy walked well out into the countryside whereupon he deemed it safe to start whistling again. It attracted three dogs. When he stopped to pat them, one bit him. God! It might have rabies!

In the doctor's surgery, he took a seat in the waiting room, every second expecting to start frothing at the mouth. No, the doctor couldn't give him an injection for rabies, as he hadn't any. Would a 'flu jab suffice?

'In any case,' said Doctor Malone, 'rabies takes forty-eight hours to incubate.'

The next forty-eight hours were hell. To overcome the waiting, Murphy went and got totally smashed. Not that he wouldn't have done just that anyway, but now he had an excuse to break the world Guinness-drinking record.

He awoke in a strange bed. Next to him was an old crone, snoring. My God! He crept out of the room only to be greeted by another crone. 'What about a kiss for the bridesmaid?' she cackled. Murphy fled the house wearing nothing but his old string vest.

The result: a high fever and 'flu. He was admitted to Sligo General Hospital where he lay in bed sweating, sweating, bloody sweating. Feck. 'Nurse! Nurse! Nurse!' Where the hell was she? For all she knew he could be dying.

'What do you want, you noisy man?' hissed the nurse. 'You've woken up half the ward.'

'I want der bed pan.'

She put it in place, but it was too late. He'd ruined it. He'd shit the bed.

'You are a terrible fellow,' said the nurse, cleaning up the mess.

'I'm sorry, Nurse, I won't do it again,' he said, covered in it.

'I'll see you don't. Next time, fever or no fever, you'll use the toilets,' she said.

THE MURPHY

'Yes, I tink dat's a reasonable suggestion. I tank you for it,' said Murphy, now reeking like the Sligo Sanitary Depot.

He had to get a bath. Still slightly delirious with the fever, Murphy reckoned that the best way to do that was to go to the council baths in Bath Street. He arrived at the door in his shit-caked hospital gown just at opening time. The attendant took one look. 'You're not coming in here dressed in that!'

An instant later he was standing naked at the door and the attendant swiftly let him in.

Lying in the warm bath, he gave a groan of relief. Bubbles rose from a fart. 'God forgive me,' he said. What a terrible experience to be covered in shit – his *own* shit. But shit and hospitals were inexorably linked in Murphy's mind.

Donald Moriarty was Chief of the Sligo Fire Brigade. It had been three years since they had had a fire. It was far too long. So, idea! There was an empty cottage just outside Sligo on the Dublin Road. One night he rode out there on his bicycle and set a slow fire burning, then hurried back to the fire station on his bike.

'Fire! Dere's a fire in der cottage on der Dublin Road!' he yelled. 'We must get dere before it goes out!'

Down the slippery pole came the firemen. They mounted the fire engine; it wouldn't start. Try as he might, Duffy the driver couldn't get the thing to start.

'Get out and push!' screamed Moriarty.

Out on the road, the thing suddenly burst into life and shot forwards, the firemen running and jumping aboard.

'We must get dere before it goes out!' howled Moriarty as they neared the Dublin Road.

Yes, there was the fire. Firemen unrolled the hosepipe, attached it to the water point. Feck! There was a leak in the hose. Moriarty clamped his hand over it. The water squirted through his fingers and drenched him. Consequently, the water pressure at the end of the hose was pathetically low and the water couldn't reach the fire. Eventually, the fire petered out of its own accord.

'Well done, lads,' called Moriarty. 'I'm proud of der way youse handled yerselves. Youse are a credit ter all of Sligo.'

Sadly, when they got back the fire station was ablaze. 'It's bloody arson!' screamed Moriarty.

Thank God the street faucet water pressure was strong and after an hour they finally managed to put the fire out. The sleeping accommodation was ruined and the firemen were put up in a ward of the Sligo General Hospital. Unfortunately, no one told the night shift nurses that they were fit and healthy firemen, so, in the middle of the night, nurses kept waking them up and making them take medicine. Next morning, they all had the shits.

This confirmed and strengthened Murphy's belief in the sinister link between hospitals and shit. Dr Malone, of course, was also a shit and Murphy hadn't seen the last of him.

Out of sympathy, Murphy went to visit his old friend Earnie Woods, who had been admitted to hospital after starting to act strangely. Some said he was mad. Some were right.

'I'm goin' ter be a giant!' screamed Earnie, springing up on to his bed and going straight through it. 'Ah, I can hear der Pope speakin' in der Vatican. Can youse hear him?'

No, Murphy couldn't hear him. 'What's he sayin'?' asked Murphy.

'I don't understand,' said Earnie. 'He's speakin' der Latin. Mae West is comin' ter see me. I'll give her der best shag she's ever had.'

Murphy decided it was time he left. 'I'll come again,' he said. As he turned, a rock hit his head.

'You won't forget, will you?' said Earnie.

'Yer bleedin' from der back of yer head,' said a nurse. 'How did yer do dat?'

'I did it by visiting Earnie Woods.'

'Oh, yes. He's known fer doin' dat sort of ting.'

'I wish I'd known,' muttered Murphy.

By the time he got home, the cut on his head was bleeding freely.

'God almighty, man, what have you done to der back of yer head?' said Molly.

'Dat lunatic Earnie Woods trew a rock at me.'

'Jesus! What did he trow it for?'

'He trew it for my head!'

'I'd better put sometin' on dat,' said Molly.

'Yes, yer nivver know where dat rock's been.'

Molly put some cold tea leaves on the wound.

'What good are dey?' moaned Murphy.

'It's my grandmudder's recipe.'

'I don't want a bloody recipe, I need medical treatment!' howled Murphy. The tea leaves were drying out fast and sprinkling down his back.

'Perhaps I'd better clean up der cut,' said Molly, washing the blood and tea leaves away.

'How big is it?' asked Murphy.

'It's about an inch long,' she said. Actually it was three inches, but she was a terrible judge of size. She thought Murphy's willy was three inches long, in fact it was nine.

29

'I'd better see der doctor,' sighed Murphy.

Leaving a trail of blood and tea leaves all the way to the doctor's surgery, Murphy presented himself before Dr Malone.

'Now this might sting a little,' said Dr Malone, a real cruel bastard.

'Oh, Christ, dat hurts!' wailed Murphy.

'Oh, not that much, man. I'm only cleaning it up a bit,' said Dr Malone, a real cruel bastard.

'What do I do wid me head now?' asked Murphy.

'Just don't wear a hat for a while,' said the real cruel bastard.

Murphy didn't have a hat, so he bought one and didn't wear it for a while.

On the way home, Murphy decided that a swift Guinness would be in order, to perk him up. In conversation with the barman, the subject of the old wishing well came up. The old wishing well was just outside Sligo and all men who drank from it were supposedly 'invigorated'. Murphy felt he could do with a bit of invigoration so, after closing time, he staggered to the wishing well. Having drunk seven pints of the invigorating water, he fell in.

It was thirty feet down and the same distance up. As the chill water struck him, it was almost cold enough to sober him up. While he was keeping himself afloat, he realised that he didn't need his hat, so he took it off.

'Dat's better,' he said, along with, 'HELPPPPP! HELPPPP! I'm drowninggggg!'

His cries went unanswered until a weakling of a man came to the well to 'invigorate' himself. 'Are you calling for help?' he shouted down to Murphy.

'Yes, it was me,' Murphy gasped. 'Fer God's sake help me up.'

'Just a minute,' said the weakling, 'I'll go and get help.'

'Fer Christ's sake hurry – I'm freezing ter death!'

The weakling returned with a rope and two of the local rugby players. One was Neil Kelly, the other was not.

'Catch hold of this,' they said, throwing the rope down.

'It doesn't reach me,' cried Murphy. 'Is there any more up your end?'

'Don't worry, we'll get some more rope!' Kelly haired off and returned with more rope, joining the two pieces together so that they reached Murphy.

'Tie it round yer waist,' they instructed. 'We'll tie it to a tree up here for safety. Now, hold on.'

The rugby boys took up the strain, and the jerk as the rope tightened threw Murphy off balance in the water. As they started to pull slowly, the rope worked its way down his legs from his waist, taking his trousers and underpants with it until it slipped all the way down to his ankles. He tried to call out, but the rope had turned him upside down and all he got was another invigorating mouthful of water.

From then on, Murphy ascended head downwards. Then, oh fuck! They lost hold of the rope sending Murphy plummeting down into the water again. Fortunately, the rope was still tied to the tree, so it didn't follow him down. They started to heave him out again, but halfway up his saviours had to stop for a rest.

'Why have you bloody stopped?' he shouted from a trouserless, upside-down position.

'We're having a rest,' they replied.

'Dere's no time for bloody resting! A man's life is at stake!' he yelled.

The time it took to haul him up seemed like an eternity to Murphy. Finally he appeared over the brim of the well, exhausted, soaked and naked from the waist down, exposing his cold and shrivelled manhood.

'Oh, tank you lads,' he gasped. 'You saved me life.'

'We all make mistakes,' they said. 'What on earth were you doing?'

'I was invigorating meself,' explained Murphy.

'Pervert!' they cried and slung him back down the well.

It was early morning before Murphy managed to haul himself back up the rope. He arrived home like a drowned rat.

'For God's sake, man, where have you been?' asked Molly.

'At der bottom of der wishing well,' he said.

'What, in God's name, were you doing down dere?' she said.

'I fell in while I was trying to invigorate meself.'

She took his soaking clothes and hung them up to dry. Murphy sat shivering by the fire. When his suit finally dried, it was two sizes too small for him. Thank God, he still had the black suit he wore for funerals.

He had hardly stepped into the street when a neighbour, Mrs Hewitt, said, 'Oh, Murphy, who's dead?'

'Nobody. I'm just wearing it to give it an airing,' he said.

He had not gone far when Tom Dickins, working on the gas board main (yet to reach Sligo Castle), said, 'Oh, Murphy, where's the funeral?'

And so on till he got indoors again.

'For God's sake where have you been this time, man?' shouted Molly.

'I bin airing me black suit, woman. Dere's nothing wrong wid dat,' he said defensively.

'But you just go out and nivver say where you're going,' she said, scratching her arse.

'Well, I don't know where I'm going until I get outside,' he said. He sat down and threw a piece of peat on the fire.

He was still feeling chilled from the episode in the wishing well. He thought about seeing the doctor, but his previous experiences with Dr Malone had not filled him with confidence in the local medical profession.

Murphy had been trying to sell a carthorse of dubious age to Terry Nolan, a dubious horse trader.

'Jesus, man, fifty pounds fer *dat*?' scoffed Nolan.

'I'm lettin' you have him cheap,' said Murphy. 'Make me an offer.'

'Two pounds,' said Nolan. 'I don't tink he will last der night.'

'Rubbish,' said Murphy. 'He's good for at least another ten rides. Two pounds? I could get that fer him fer dog food.'

'Yes, dat's what I'm buyin' him fer,' said Nolan, patting the horse.

'Don't do dat, he'll fall over,' warned Murphy. 'I'll withdraw him from der sale. I'll send him to a home for old horses to end his days in peace.'

'God, man,' said Nolan, 'he'll never last the journey.'

'Well, dat's up to him,' said Murphy, and he helped the nag back to the stable. Alas, on the way there, the horse collapsed and died.

'Okay, two pounds and he's yours,' said Murphy. Two pounds was better than nothing was, but only just.

'Two bloody pounds?' said Molly, when Murphy arrived home.

'It was a good price fer a dead horse.'

'Der horse was alive when I saw it,' she said.

'Yes, but he died during der bidding. Der buyer was just about ter up der price,' said Murphy.

'Oh, what a bloody time to die!' said Molly. 'How old was he?'

'He was about fifty-tree.'

'Not der buyer, you eejit, der horse.'

'I don't know,' said Murphy, 'but he won't be gettin' any older now.'

'Dat horse was alive when my farder was alive,' said Molly, pouring a mass of chopped vegetables on a boiling brown stew.

'What is dat?' asked Murphy.

'It's a Greek dish,' she lied.

'Yes, but what's in it?' insisted Murphy, unimpressed.

'It's a sort of ragout.'

'What's dat?'

'It's French for stew.' Finally she had to admit that they were having stew again, but Murphy had been totally distracted.

'Don't talk to me about dem feckin' French! When me and der lads was on leave in Paris during der war, dey would spit at us. Dey were terrible shots, dey always missed. And dem Paris girls only went wid der 'Mericans. Serves dem bloody right, dey all got der veneral. Dat's a terrible ting, dat is. You feel as if yer balls are on fire. We didn't have much money, so we would walk der streets and whistle. You can't do much wrong doin' dat.'

'What about dat Moulin Rouge place,' asked Molly, stirring the boiling mess of stew. It got worse with every stir. Eventually, Murphy would have to eat it.

'Oh, dat was closed down,' he said.

'From what I heard it was clothes off,' she laughed, the spit from it landing in the stew.

34

THE MURPHY

'When do we eat, darlin'?' asked Murphy, seating himself at the table and tucking a dirty napkin into his collar. He held a knife and fork in his hands expectantly. An hour later he was still sitting there.

'For God's sake, woman, how long will youse be?' he wailed.

'Five foot six,' she said. She transferred the steaming saucepan to a spot in front of Murphy. 'Dere, help yerself,' she said, lighting up cigarette and inhaling a lungful of life-shortening tobacco smog.

'You know dat smokin' is bad fer you,' warned Murphy, helping himself to a plateful of terrible, terrible stew.

Yes, but smoking was the only pleasure she had since he had stopped shagging her.

'Youse know dat yer lungs are black,' he said.

'No, I can't see dem from here,' she replied.

'I hope,' he said, 'I die before you do.'

'Why?' she asked.

'Because I want to.'

He took a spoon to the hellish, hellish stew, took a mouthful, immediately clutched his throat, stood up and fell sideways in slow motion.

'Molly, call der doctor,' he gasped.

'All right,' said Molly, 'but he won't eat it either.'

Dr Malone came. 'Sorry I'm late,' he said, 'but I was operating on a cat's hernia. Now, Murphy, what appears to be the trouble?'

'It's der stew, Doc, dere's sometin' in it.'

'All stews have something in it, man.'

'It's burnin' me troat,' gasped Murphy, still clutching his throat.

'Oh, it's der chillies, Doctor,' explained Molly. 'I put quite a lot of dem in.'

'Dat's it, Doc,' groaned Murphy, 'It's der chilli poison-ing.'

'A glass of water should do the trick,' said the doctor.

Molly filled a glass with water, brought it over and threw it in Murphy's face.

'There, now,' said the doctor. 'Isn't that better?'

For the good of his health and to keep him away from bloody doctors, Murphy decided to look for a job. He went to the police station and asked if they had enough policemen. Yes, they did. Feck. He went to the convent and asked if they needed an odd job. They already had one. Feck. He went to the Army Recruitment Centre and tried to join up again. He lied about his age; he said he was eighteen. They said don't be such a bloody fool. Feck. By now it was getting late, so he went to the pub and ordered a drink on credit. His bill stood at £320.

'When are yer goin' ter pay it, Murphy?' asked the barman.

'Look, let's start by me workin' off some of der debt,' said Murphy. 'Youse could use my labour.'

They took him at his word. Soon he was unloading huge barrels of Guinness. It gave him a hernia. He was operated on in Sligo General by Dr Malone.

'Will youse be careful when yer down dere, Doc?' pleaded Murphy. 'They're all I've got.'

'We'll certainly be careful,' said the doctor, 'because you *do* have a lot down there.' He stared at Murphy's huge willy and carthorse bollocks.

So Murphy's Guinness-loading days were over, but he had cleared his bar bill. Shame he had to get a hernia to do it. Feck.

Making a gentle recovery, Murphy got a job on a farm as a shepherd. He wore gumboots because of the mud and sheep shit and had a collie dog to help him. He stood all bloody day in the freezing bloody cold looking after the sheep, and not a bleat of thanks from them. He caught pneumonia. Feck! He was back in Sligo General with a raging temperature.

'It's called the old man's frost,' smiled Dr Malone, 'because it takes you away so quiet and cold during the night.'

Feck.

Murphy awoke one morning in the hospital to find a sheet drawn over his head. My God, was he dead? He called a nurse. She came and pulled the sheet from his face. He asked her if he was dead. She said no, but that morning he had seemed partly dead, so they pulled the sheet over him just in case.

Murphy was delighted at being alive, it was much better than being dead. He went back to sleep again and awoke to find the sheet pulled over him again. He called the nurse.

'Oh,' she said. 'Still with us, then? We only did it as a precaution to save time later.'

Despite all the combined efforts of the finest of Sligo's medical fraternity, Murphy stubbornly refused to die.

To convalesce, they sent him to a holiday camp. It was winter and deserted. He was shown to a wooden hut, which was very comfortable inside. He immediately lay on the bed and fell asleep. When he awoke, to his great relief, he was not covered by a sheet. It was night time. Dinner, where did you get it?

The camp area was floodlit and he soon found the restaurant. The menu was brief and they didn't serve food after nine-thirty. As it was after nine-thirty, Murphy asked if he could have a cheese sandwich? No, after nine-thirty they only served ham. He took it and was charged two shillings. On the way back to his hut he tried to sell it to a stranger without much success. As it was now his only major asset, he swallowed it for safety.

Next morning, he had fried egg and bacon. That was three shillings. Would they take one shilling and ten pence? They asked why. He told them, 'Because it's all I've got.' They took it. Feck.

With no money left, he decided it was time to go home.

'Where in God's name have you been, man?' Molly bawled the traditional greeting.

'Walking back from der bloody holiday camp.'

'What in God's name were you doin' dere?'

'I was convalescing from pneumonia.'

'How in God's name did yer get dat?'

Even Murphy, who never really listened to what his wife had to say, was beginning to find her conversation somewhat repetitive. 'Workin' as a shepherd,' he said.

'What in God's name was you doin' as a bloody shepherd.'

'Lookin' after der sheep.' It seemed the obvious answer.

'Well,' said Molly, 'der man from der Army came and he said youse could join up as a senior citizen reserve. Youse have ter report to dem dis mornin'.'

Murphy reported to the Army Depot and was ushered into a long wooden hut where a doctor awaited him.

'Strip off,' he said.

'Shouldn't you ask me out to dinner or sometin' first?' asked Murphy.

'How long has it been like that?'

'Dat's as long as it's ever been,' said Murphy.

The doctor made a note on a chart and a sergeant appeared.

'Draw yer uniform from the stores!' barked the sergeant.

Murphy was issued with his uniform and tried it on.

'It's miles too big,' he complained.

'Well, it's he best we can do,' said the sergeant.

Wearing his new uniform, Murphy somehow made it to the new arrivals holding area. 'Is somebody in there?' asked an officer, addressing the huge uniform.

'Private Murphy, 954024,' said Murphy, unable to see out and facing in entirely the wrong direction.

That day he was dishonourably discharged as totally useless. Feck!

Maybe it was something about being in uniform again, no matter how big it was, or maybe it was the amount of time that Murphy had spent in hospital that inspired him to go looking for a job at Sligo General. He thought he might be too old to start learning how to be a doctor, but he certainly wasn't too old to be a nursing orderly.

'Yes, we'll be glad to have you, we're short of orderlies,' said the matron. 'You'll have to have a shave first, then change into the orderly's uniform.'

So he was back in uniform. His first job was wheeling a corpse to the bank of refrigerated drawers in the morgue.

'You have to put the identification label on his toe,' explained the matron.

'But he's dead,' said Murphy. 'How will I get his name?'

'The almoner will tell you,' said the Matron.

Where was the bloody almoner? He found her a mile away in a separate building. 'I got ter get der stiff's name from youse,' said Murphy.

'The stiff? Do you mean the deceased?' asked the almoner.

'Yes, der deceased stiff,' said Murphy.

'Where did you bring him from?' asked the almoner.

'Der operatin' teater,' said Murphy.

'That would be Thomas Kuspinski,' said the almoner.

'I can't spell dat,' frowned Murphy.

The almoner wrote it down for him. Murphy fixed the label to the deceased's toe, then slid the stiff into a refrigerated drawer. He wished the stiff Good Luck, although it was patently too late. All day he wheeled stiffs in and out, quickly becoming thoroughly disillusioned with his new medical career.

'Dere's no future in dis,' he muttered, sliding a female corpse into the refrigeration unit and giving her tits a farewell rub. There were several more like her and, before he became a necrophile, he left.

Murphy realised that, at thirteen stone, he was overweight for a man of five foot seven and a half. Right! He would start right away: no more potatoes, cream, butter, sugar, chocolate and peas. Why peas? Why not? He stuck to his diet for a week. He lost three pounds. He stuck to it for another week. He lost another pound. Total, four pounds. 'Dat's enough!' he thought, returning to his normal diet of potatoes, cream, butter, sugar, chocolate and peas. Why peas? Why not? He weighed himself. He was thirteen stone, the right weight for a man of five foot seven and a half.

That night he saw himself nude in the mirror. He had to lie down. God, he was a terrible shape! Was he deformed? With that, he fell asleep. When he awoke he was still the same shape.

40

In distant Bombay, Dr Cursages was also still the same shape and attending his surgery. His patient was recovering from smallpox and him. He had given the man a powerful laxative of local manufacture called Shitzlit. For the next thirty-six hours the patient, Percy Lalbakar, sat on the toilet. Eventually, he fainted. His wife, Mungalabai, found him unconscious, slumped against the porcelain. She did the best she could. She threw a bucket of cold water over him.

'Woman, what are you doing?' he screamed as he came round.

'I'm trying to make you better,' she said.

Poor Percy Lalbakar. He was a Nappi (barber) attached to the Royal West Kents stationed at Ghorpur Barracks, Poona. It was a well-paid job for a local. Recovering from small pox, he was on convalescence at the end of the old Sappers Lines, the barracks accommodation that was the residence of his widowed mother, Mrs Aida Tin-Tin, who had married a British soldier, a West Kents bandsman.

Bandsman Tin-Tin had been killed when a tree he had been sheltering under fell on him. Nobody knew he was there. He was discovered by Bookajee, whose job it was to count the trees in the cantonment. When he went to count this one it had fallen down. Under it he found Bandsman Tin-Tin. He looked as if he was dead. He not only looked it, he *was* dead. Bookajee called the local hospital and they sent an ambulance and a stretcher. They put Bandsman Tin-Tin on the stretcher but he had been squashed so flat that the slightest breeze lifted him up and blew him off again, so they had to weight him down with stones.

At his funeral Bandsman Tin-Tin was buried with full military honours: The Last Post was played and the Union

41

Jack was draped over a very thin coffin. His wife threw a handful of soil on the coffin; a hard bit split the lid. It was the final indignity of his short life, ended by a tree. His wife wanted to keep the tree as a memorial; alas, too late, the tree had been cut up and stacked as logs for firewood. Bandsman Tin-Tin's tombstone read 'Killed by a tree for his King and Country'.

Murphy learned of this tragedy from his friend, Terence O'Toole, the inspector for the Sligo Gas Board, who came by for a chat, sitting himself down on the edge of Murphy's bed.

'And how are youse gettin' on, Murphy?'

Well, Murphy was getting on. He was getting on for fifty-six. 'Dere's nuttin' you can do when you're fifty-six,' he said.

'Why, Murphy, you're in your prime. Life is just startin' for you,' assured O'Toole.

That was news to Murphy.

'Have youse ever been ter Portugal?' said O'Toole.

'I don't tink so,' said Murphy, thinking that it must be someplace up north, or possibly in India. 'If I have, I've forgotten. Why?'

'Me and me wife are goin' dere on holiday,' said O'Toole. 'A place called Park des Roches. I'm lookin' forward to it.'

'Well, now. It would be silly to look backwards to it,' said Murphy. 'How long will you be dere?'

'Der same as I am here, five foot eleven,' said O'Toole.

Murphy frowned. That wasn't the answer he wanted, but he wouldn't press it further in case it became obvious that he had no idea where Portugal was. Thankfully, O'Toole left to inspect some gas, or whatever it was he did.

'Are youse goin' ter lie all day in bloody bed?' yelled Molly.

THE MURPHY

'I'll get up soon,' he answered her.

Soon was two hours later, and opening time. Murphy watched as the barman, ever so carefully, drew a Guinness. It took him a whole minute. Murphy held it up like the communion chalice. This was the greatest drink in the world. Mind you, he had never drunk anything else, except in the war in France when he had drunk nothing else but cheap wine. He had slept with a French slapper and caught the clap. He recalled it was worth it. The medical officer gave shots of penicillin to everyone who had caught it. At one time twenty per cent of the Allied soldiers were down with it. Somehow what was left won the war.

Now that he thought about it, Portugal was somewhere near France wasn't it? Or was it in Africa? He left the bar when his money ran out and walked down the street to draw his dole money. Thank God Molly had a job in the chemist or they'd have starved by now. He thought of the poor in Africa starving. The world was full of hungry people and he would soon be one of them, but he'd be saved, thanks to Irish stew. How the hungry in Africa would love a good Irish stew. They probably wouldn't know a good Irish stew if they saw one. Mind you, the way Molly cooked, neither would he. He was certain, though, that no African had ever seen any kind of Irish stew. Feck their luck, poor devils.

Oh, yes, the world was a big place. What was happening on the other side of it? Australia. Bluey Hewitt was hungry. He was tracking a 'roo. The bugger was somewhere in the bloody bush. He could hear him but he couldn't see him and, if he couldn't see him, he couldn't shoot him. Shit.

Maybe if he shot where he thought he was? Yes, that's it. Bang! Followed by a human scream. He had shot a fellow hunter in the arse.

'You bloody fool!' screamed the victim, Bruce Swagman.

'Gee, I'm sorry, mate,' said Bluey.

'*You're* sorry?' wailed Bruce. 'I've just had half me arse shot away!'

'Naw, I only winged you, mate,' lied Bluey. 'Here, take some of these.'

'What in Christ are they?'

'Painkillers.'

'Are they any good?' asked Bruce, swallowing a handful.

'Seemed to work fine for me uncle's horse,' said Bluey.

Bruce blinked. Nothing happened. He swallowed a couple more pills. Then a strange, glazed look came into his eyes, he stood dead still with an awkward, sagging stance and his face fell as slack as the arse of Bluey's shorts.

'You all right, mate?' asked Bluey. 'How's the pain?'

'What pain?' yelled Bruce, suddenly springing back to life. 'There's no time for pain on this submarine!' He rushed off into the bush, making whooping noises. 'Dive! Dive! Dive! How do you get out of this car park? Mind that octopus!'

Bluey was so impressed he took a couple of the painkillers himself. Just then the kangaroo jumped out of the bush in front of him. He levelled his gun at it and tracked its hopping motion across the clearing, finally taking a pot shot when he was on an up bounce. He lost his balance and blew the branch off a tree overhead. The branch poleaxed him and the last thing he heard before he lost consciousness was 'Up periscope . . .!'

Of course, Murphy, now safely back in the Sligo pub clutching his dole money, knew nothing of this. He didn't even know what a kangaroo was but then, neither did Captain Cook until an Aborigine told him. Still, he was able to muse over what a strange world it was, especially for Catholics. 'Yes,' thought Murphy, 'der religion makes dis strange old world even stranger . . .'

Religion

Chapter 4

Murphy was one of five brothers born to Elizabeth and William Murphy of 5 Holborn Street, Sligo. The family was desperately poor. The five boys were all shabbily dressed, so much so that when Father Finlay came to call, Elizabeth gave the boys a plate of bread and butter and hid them in the bedroom.

The priest arrived. Elizabeth had laid out a high tea for him and a glass of Jameson's. After an hour, a voice came from the bedroom: 'More bread and butter, or we come out, shabby clothes and all!'

Now Father Finlay was a rare priest. He boxed for the Sligo Boys' Club at 14 stone 6 pounds. He was due to fight the English amateur heavyweight, Jim Slade. The fight would take place at the People's Palace in Collins Square.

'How do yer fancy yer chances, Farder?' asked William.

'Murphy, I think the result will be the will of God,' said the priest.

'God? How about der judges?' said William.

'Oh, they'll have a say,' said the priest, swallowing a mouthful of Jameson's.

'I wouldn't rely too much on God, Farder,' advised William. 'Do you train on dat stuff?' He pointed at the whiskey.

'As much as I can,' said the priest.

'So do I,' said William, 'but I'm not goin' into der ring to fight.'

'I notice you're not going to confession, either,' counter-ed the priest. 'You haven't been for some time.'

'No,' said William. 'I'm stayin' away till I've got enough to confess.'

'More bread and butter or we come down shabby clothes and all!'

Under threat, Elizabeth hastily buttered some bread and slid the plate under the door. In a flash the plate was empty. 'Now shut up,' said Elizabeth, 'or yer farder will tie you all to the bed.'

For Murphy's parents, their fear of embarrassment was far greater than their fear of God. But then, why should any of us fear God, thought Murphy? Who in hell was God? Nobody, but nobody seemed to know. 'He's in Heaven,' they would say. Well where the bloody hell was Heaven, eh? Where? Where was God? What did the bugger look like? No, nobody could say. In fact, no sane person knew where He was or what He looked like. So, basically, there was not a God. People just went around believing in Him. Why Him? Why not Her? Why not a homosexual? No, 'they' wanted God to be perfection itself. It was all bollocks; there was no God. Could you say that to anybody? Say it to a priest and he would collapse. And it had been going on since time began. Essentially, man could not live in a world where death was the end. No, man wanted a second chance in somewhere called Heaven where he could dwell eternally. When they were dying they would fortify their last moments, calling for the priest to give them extreme extra absolution, a sort of spiritual armour to help them access Heaven. Oh, the silly fools! Billions of them lay buried, never having gone *anywhere*!

Nobody could accuse Murphy of never having gone anywhere. In fact, he had travelled far and wide in the name of religion. His first religious journey began one night as he staggered from the pub.

Closin' time is a threat to mankind, he thought. He stopped in a quiet lane to rest. A blinding light suddenly burst in front of him and a strange-shaped object settled down a few feet from him, coloured lights flashing on its roof.

Then came an amplified Irish voice: 'Mick Murphy, prepare to meet St Patrick.'

A sloping walkway was lowered from an illuminated doorway and a man appeared, wearing a flashing boiler suit and cap. He beckoned Murphy to come forward. A magnetic force drew Murphy towards the craft.

'Mick, come inside for a Guinness,' said the voice, finishing with a fit of sneezing.

Inside the flashing craft there was a peat fire burning beneath an ornate mantelpiece. Several customers, all in shabby clothes, leaned against a well-stocked bar.

'It's bin a very bad year for us. Dere isn't much money about, so we have to make do wid borrowing from der bank,' said the man in the flashing boiler suit. 'Come in, man, dere's a terrible draught coming under the door.'

Once Murphy was inside, the craft started to take off with an electrical whine. Murphy looked out of the window. Jesus, dere below he could see his own home.

'Listen,' he said to the barman, 'my missus is expecting me home soon.'

'Oh, we'll take you home after you've met St Patrick. Have a jar while you're here.'

Dis is better, thought Murphy. In fact, he said it. 'Dis is better,' said Murphy, swallowing a Guinness.

A television set lit up; on screen there appeared a man in a boiler suit with a halo. 'Hi dere, Murphy.' Who was this silly bugger?

'Dat's Saint Patrick,' said the man in the illuminated boiler suit.

'Is dat right?' said Murphy. 'Is he der same feller dat drove all of der snakes out of Ireland in a van?'

Yes, he was.

'I'm waitin' for der National Lottery numbers,' said Saint Patrick. 'God knows, I need der bloody money.'

'Is dat right?' said Murphy. 'God knows?'

'Yes,' said Saint Patrick, 'so I'm in wid a chance. Be just my bloody luck to see a Proddy win. Now, Murphy, would you like an autographed photograph of me in me robes?'

'Oh, yes. Twill be worth a fortune. Der local priest would be mad not to buy it.'

'Now, Murphy, first we have to operate on you for a grumbling appendix.' Oh, Lord, even his appendix was grumbling, although Murphy hadn't really noticed.

In an instant he was in the operating theatre. By the operating table was one surgeon holding a pickaxe, another holding a shovel.

'Don't worry, youse won't feel a ting,' they said, making him drink a bottle of Jameson's.

When it was over, the vehicle dropped him at a bus stop.

'Where have you been, man?' said Molly.

'I was taken up by an Irish flying saucer,' Murphy explained, settling by the fire.

'Youse is pissed,' she retorted.

'No! It's der truth, Molly.'

'Oh, where did dey take you?'

'Dey took me to a bus stop,' he said, poking the fire.

'Have you reported dis to der police?' asked Molly, clearly unconvinced.

'Dey took my appendix out, Molly,' he said.

'Well dat'll save youse havin' ter be done again.'

The bloody papers didn't believe him, either: '*The man in question, Mr Michael Murphy, when interviewed by the police, swore he was a teetotaller, but a blood sample showed him to be seventeen times over the limit. The police dismissed his story as spurious.*'

Well, they might not believe him, but Murphy remembered the flying saucer well. While it was on the ground, a member of the crew repainted it. It was supposed to make the saucer invisible, but it must have been the wrong paint because Murphy could still see it. He also remembered that part of the saucer was rented out to a family who were homeless. They charged them a pound a week in rent. The flying saucer had even given him a contact number. He phoned from a call box. It was out of order. Apparently, they hadn't paid their phone bill.

Dat figures, thought Murphy. Irish flying saucers is very short of cash. Dey had to borrow ten million pounds from der bank. Der loan must have come tru too late to stop dem cuttin' off der phone.

Murphy hadn't got a phone. If he wanted to speak to a neighbour, he'd shout out the window. If they couldn't hear him, he'd stand in the road and shout. He was frequently run over by a bus – and then discovered he could get compensation from the bus company. Eventually, the bus found it cheaper to drive *round* him. Now that the buses were missing him, Murphy was missing the money and, while it wasn't much fun being knocked down by a bus, in time he had grown used to it. When they started to drive round him he suffered withdrawal symptoms. He had to have counselling and go through withdrawal therapy, where he was repeatedly run over by ever smaller vehicles starting with a lorry, then a van, then a family saloon car, then a motorcycle and sidecar combination and finally a child's pram. By the end of it he was completely cured and half-dead.

Murphy's second religious journey was somewhat more conventional. It was Ash Wednesday and he had to go to Mass.

Ash Wednesday, said Murphy to himself. Why do we have ter go ter Mass and have der ashes on der forehead. What a lot of idiots dey all look, walking about wid ashes on their foreheads. What a bloody religion. Fish on Friday. God, dey can't afford fish from Monday till Thursday, dey live off cheap cuts from der butchers and tripe. But dere's always plenty of bloody potatoes. You got potatoes wid everytin'. You got potatoes wid potatoes! Why was Ireland so poor? Dere was always enough potatoes to go round.'

As luck would have it, this was one Ash Wednesday Mass Murphy was glad not to miss. The senior Catholics of Sligo were going on a 'free' trip to Rome, paid for out of Church Funds, funded by the poor of the parish. It would be wonderful to see the Pope.

Despite his experience in the flying saucer, Murphy didn't like flying. Mind you, flying wasn't dangerous . . . crashing was dangerous. Oh, but it would all be worth it to talk to His Holiness the Pope.

Murphy's audience with the Pope was a short-lived affair: 'Hello, Holy Farder, how is youse gettin' on? How is der wife and kids?'

'Very well, my son. How are you?'

'Oh, me, Farder? I'm fine, Farder. Now me wife, Molly, has asked me ter get yer autograph on dis photo of her mudder.'

Dutifully, the Pope signed Molly's mother's photograph.

'Tank you, Holy Farder. Good luck on you.'

The Pope moved away from him, working his way through the crowds of people. Murphy never saw him again. Still, when you've seen one Pope, you've seen 'em all.

Murphy visited a restaurant in Rome, determined to do as the Romans do. He ordered spaghetti bolognese, which he ate with a knife and fork; it took him nearly an hour and a half. When asked by the waiter what he would like for dessert, he replied, 'I'd like rhubarb and custard.' The waiter denied all knowledge of rhubarb, so Murphy ordered 'sumtin' sweet' and wound up with the waitress.

Oh, it's great to be in Rome. [he wrote to Molly] *The weather is lovely. I'm staying in a B&B. The trouble is, as soon as you've had your breakfast, they make you bugger off. Not having much money, you walk the streets all day. By 8 o'clock I feel buggered and am glad to get to bloody bed. I try to go to sleep quickly before I feel hungry.*

I've been all over the Vatican. There's fellers here selling pieces of the original cross. I bought a piece for you. It is a genuine relic, blessed by the Pope, made in Taiwan.

Last night I went to see Madam Butterfly. *This time they didn't all slide to the front of the stage, so it wasn't as funny.*

The girls here are not allowed out alone. They all have a feller with them so they don't feel lonely. I went to talk to one and the feller told me to go away. I told him I was a Roman Catholic

and he still told me to go away. So I knocked him down. He got
up and knocked me down. A policeman arrested us both and put
us in a cell. Next morning we were up before the judge – he got
up an hour later. He fined us a hundred lire. I asked for time to
pay; he said now was the time to pay. I gave him a ten thousand
lire note and he asked if I had anything smaller, so I gave him a
button off my shirt. He gave me two hundred lire change.
    I'll soon be home,
    love, Mick

When Murphy got home to Sligo, Molly was beside herself
with joy at her presents, especially the signed photograph
of her mother.

'Oh, 'twas lovely of der dear man,' she said, crossing
herself. Why not? She crossed everyone else. Then she
kissed the photo and said they'd get a fortune for it.

Next week at Crosby auction gallery, it was among the
items for sale. It was mounted in a white plastic frame,
which had cost Murphy £3.00. It went for £3.00.

'Youse are bloody useless, man,' was Molly's comment.
'God knows why I married you.'

'Because I'm a good shag,' he retorted.

She hesitated. Yes, he was a good shag. *Was* was the
operative word there. He hadn't given her much pleasure
recently. Occasionally she used a dill-doll ten inches long.
It was a sin in the Catholic church. 'Feck der Catholic
Church,' she muttered as she inserted the dill-doll. God it
was cold, she should have warmed it up in the oven.

She could hear Murphy singing in the bath:

What is a dill-doll, Daddy?
Said my little daughter of nine.

THE MURPHY

A dill-doll my chick
Is a properly prick
Ten times the size of mine.
Your mother had one for Christmas
Straight off the Christmas tree
She's used it but twice
And found it so nice
She's no bloody use for me.

'Dat's a disgusting song,' said Molly. 'You'll have ter go
ter confession and tell dat ter Farder Brenan.'

'Why?' asked Murphy. 'He won't like it either. He'll
probably give me a tousand Hail Marys.'

So he did a thousand Hail Marys. It took Murphy till
midnight to finish them.

'Where in God's name have you been, man?' said Molly,
putting his dinner on the table.

'What's dis?' he said.

'It's bean stew,' she replied.

'Never mind what it's been, what is it now?'

A thousand Hail Marys for singing a naughty song. That
must be in *The Guinness Book of Records*. He phoned them the
next morning. They said it wasn't a record, some poor
bugger had been given two thousand. He must have known
the second verse. Feck.

To temper his disappointment, Murphy sought out his
friend Madigan, who always had a good tip on the horses.

'I got a tip fer der Irish Derby,' said the tout Madigan.
'It's Frosty Day. Der odds are very good, 100–1, but you
better hurry before dey change.'

Murphy managed to get those odds. He put the £3.00
from the picture auction on the horse. December the tird,

57

Derby Day, the tree o'clock race. Murphy stood near the rail at the winning post. There were twenty-one runners. As they entered the straight, yes, yes, yes, there was Frosty Day . . . last.

'Wait till I see dat bastard Madigan.' Murphy waited and waited, but he never saw him again.

How much disappointment can one man take? Murphy was desperately unhappy and needed some way of lifting his black mood. A novena! Yes, his mudder had once gone on such a religious retreat to pray to the Virgin Mary. She'd come back very happy.

Murphy asked Father Brenan about it. He would have to go to the Monastery of Bray, just outside Sligo, where he would be welcomed by the Christian Brothers de la Salle. So began Murphy's third religious journey.

He was met at the monastery by Brother Theopholipus, a German. 'Ach, velcome to zer monasztery. Your novena starts tomorrow, nein?'

Murphy was shown to his cell – ten foot by six, with a wooden bed and three blankets.

'Ve avake at dawn, zen ve all say prayers in zer main hall. Zen breakfast of black bread and water, ja?'

Was this feller out of his mind? No. At dawn a brother shook him awake and gave him a long brown shift to put on. Half asleep, he knelt in the main hall and found himself yawning and praying. All the prayers were said in Latin. He remembered the odd Latin word from Mass and filled in when there was a place for it.

Then the senior brother spoke. 'For the rest of the day, there will be no speaking unless there is an emergency.'

Well, Murphy had an emergency all right. He needed a shit but didn't know where to go. 'Where is der lavatory?' he whispered to a brother. The brother didn't answer, he pointed outdoors. Murphy went that way, and found what passed for a lavatory – God, he had never seen a contraption like it. A wooden seat with a bucket underneath and a bucket with a handle, full of sand.

'Ah, dat's der stuff yer sprinkles over der crap.'

Murphy was beginning to think that the novena hadn't been such a good idea. At least when he was taken away by the Irish flying saucer and lost his appendix, they had modern facilities. He went back to his cell, lay on the wooden bed, covered himself with blankets and tried to sleep. Not for long. A brother came in and beckoned him to follow. It was Mass, said in silence. A brother read the Gospel but never spoke it. Afterwards, Murphy waited in his cell for lunch. He was given a plate of potatoes and a glass of water. A brother indicated that they grew them. If dey grew on me, I'd chop dem off, thought Murphy. A hard, unripe Granny Smith apple was dessert, then, by God, exercise in the garden: stretch and bend, arms swinging, running on the spot.

Feck! thought Murphy, but he hadn't experienced the cold showers yet. Look at his bollocks! They had shrunk to the size of peanuts! He had to wait a full hour before they returned to their normal size of a carthorse. It was his secret.

Supervised gardening, planting bloody seeds in the pouring rain. As the brother said, 'Rain, rain, blessed, blessed rain.' Yes, the blessed, blessed rain – Murphy was soaked with it. He started to sneeze, sneeze, blessed, blessed sneeze. God help him he might have caught bronchitis. No, not *might* have, *had* caught it! Feck. He could die from this. He waited. He did not die from it, but he spent three weeks coughing up what looked like raw eggs.

He returned from the novena even more unhappy than he had been before he left and decided to counter this by improving his mind. He went to the County Library.

'Have youse got a book on der Virgin birth?' he asked.

'No, sor, it's out.'

'Has it been out long?' asked Murphy.

'Yes, nine months. We have written asking her to return it.'

'It's a woman, den,' said Murphy. 'Now why should a woman want to keep a book on der Virgin birth fcɪ ɪɪɪɪɪɪe months?"

It was a mystery that was beyond Murphy's limited powers of comprehension. The only woman he could remember having a Virgin Birth was Mary, mother of Jesus. The poor woman had never had a decent shag. Jesus had a foster father. 'He's no bloody use to me,' said Jesus. 'I want a father that shags!'

What a terrible way for a nice man ter die, thought Murphy. Crucified. Oh, if only Jesus had a good Jewish solicitor, he'd have had him down off der cross on notice of appeal and ended up wid only a small fine and time ter pay.

Still, it was too late for that now. Oh, that man Jesus, they say he could walk on the water. What a lot of balls; he would have drowned. No one can walk on water. Murphy's father was a good Catholic. He believed that Jesus could walk on the water. One night when he'd had a skinful he went to Sligo Bay. They rowed him a mile off shore and he got out of the boat to walk to shore. He went straight to the bloddy bottom, silly bugger. He had to have mouth to mouth resuscitation – they had to pay a bloke to do it. That was another thing that Jesus could do – raise the dead. What a waste of time, one day they would only go and die again.

THE MURPHY

Father Brenan was impressed with Murphy's attempts to better himself.

'Remember, Murphy,' he said, 'the world is your oyster.'

'What is my oyster, Farder?' said Murphy.

'Why, the world, Murphy,' repeated the priest. 'It's a philosophical saying.'

'Well, it makes no bloody sense to me,' said Murphy.

'That's because you are unread,' said the priest.

'I'm not red?' queried Murphy. 'I know I'm not red, I can see dat!'

'Forget it, Murphy,' said the priest. So Murphy forgot it.

The priest had a disturbing story to tell about the dear Pope. The Pope's medical advisor had noticed that the Pope's spirits were very low. What the Pope needed was a good shag. He advised the Pope to indulge in a little sexual pleasure. The Pope was horrified.

'No, no, my son. Never, never, never.'

The advisor insisted and gradually the Pope wilted. Yes, but who in god's name would sleep with him? The medical advisor was ready for that one.

'Holy Father, a small group of nurses are willing to sacrifice themselves. See here are some photographs of them. You must choose one.'

The dear Pope scanned the photographs, then said, 'I'll have the one with the big tits.'

The Sligo Zoo. That was worth a visit to improve his mind. Cage one was a carthorse. Cage two was a cow and her calf. Next was a pig, then a goat, then a rabbit, then an empty cage with a sign: AWAITING DELIVERY OF A LION OR AN ELEPHANT, SIGNED, ANDREW MOSS, ZOO DIRECTOR

61

A general sign read DO NOT FEED THE ANIMALS – THEY ARE NOT HUNGRY. Well, the animals might not be hungry, but Murphy certainly was.

He left the zoo and called in at the Convent of Jesus and Mary.

'Oh, Mudder Superior, do you have any food? Yer see, I have of a sudden got der hunger.'

'My dear man, come inside. Sister Fabien will fix you up with a curry.'

Curry was the meal of the day. They sat him down in the refectory and set a curry before him. Murphy had never eaten a curry. Feck! It was the school lunch break. Soon he was surrounded by fourteen-year-old girls. Of course, this was a girls' school!

'Who are you, sir?' asked one girl.

'I'm Michael Murphy,' was all he could think to say.

'What are you doing here?'

Rather than admit he was begging, Murphy explained that the nuns had cooked too much curry and had asked him to eat the surplus. How did the swine get away with it? He polished off his curry as quickly as he could. God he could do with a good shit; the curry had activated his bowels. He made a dash for the toilets. Flinging open the door of one cubicle, he was greeted with a scream and a small girl seated on the loo. Why didn't she lock the door? Of course, bloody fool, 'twas a girls' school and the last thing they would expect was a desperate man rampaging through the toilets. Thank God it wasn't a nun sitting there.

He made his way out of the convent and headed straight for the public toilet. Feck – closed! He'd have to hold it in till he got home.

Bloody hell! His wife was on it! The strain was becoming too much to bear. No wonder people committed suicide, although he couldn't remember hearing of anyone who had committed suicide because they couldn't get a shit. Well he wasn't going to stand for it.

'Hurry up in dere, woman!' he screamed, banging on the door.

'God, man, can't a woman do a shit in peace?' said Molly, with a strain in her voice.

Murphy rested against the doorpost and a radio advertising slogan sprang to mind. 'Housewives, do you want your toilet sparkling clean? Then do it in the garden!' Not quite the jingle the advertisers had in mind, but not a bad slogan. He went off and did it in the garden, then blamed the poor bloody dog. Mind you, it was a splendid effort that any dog would have been proud of. Someone would have their work cut out clearing up that feller.

'Work,' sighed Murphy, 'is der curse of der drinking classes . . .'

Work

Chapter 5

Showing at the local cinema was a silent film of *Tarzan*, played by Frank Edwards, an actor with a magnificent torso, but painfully thin legs. This they overcame by having him wear a long leopard skin back and front from the waist down. In the film, Tarzan manfully strangled a gorilla with his bare hands and also killed a lion that was stuffed.

A newsreel followed, showing strikes in America.

'Ah, America!' sighed Murphy. 'Dat's der place fer strikes.'

His uncle had gone to America and become a policeman. He married a huge German woman who beat the shit out of him every night.

'America's der land of opportunity!' exclaimed Murphy, as he and Molly walked home.

'Den why don't you go dere?' asked Molly.

'I don't want an opportunity,' he answered. 'I might not like it . . . I won't be a moment,' he added, disappearing into a public toilet.

He swiftly reappeared. 'Oh, what a filthy mess! None of the dirty buggers had pulled der chain.'

He reported the condition to the Council Sanitary Officer, Adam Ripley, who immediately went round and pulled all the chains – a man of action. Murphy admired that. He determined to become a man of action and took a new job at The Sligo Funeral Parlour. He had to show customers the entire range of coffins, from the reinforced cardboard 'Powell', to the mahogany 'Churchill'. He sold a lot of 'Powells' but never a 'Churchill'.

'People can't afford to die in style these days,' he said, sadly. He was on commission.

Mrs Priscilla Doyle came seeking a coffin for her husband.

'Is he dead?' asked Murphy.

'No, he's not,' she said, 'but I don't want to leave it till the last moment.'

In fact, Mr Doyle was only 23. She chose the 'Powell'. It was put on the back of an open-topped lorry and driven back to her house in the rain. When they arrived, the cardboard had softened and collapsed.

'It'll be all right when it dries out,' Murphy advised by phone. 'Put it in front of der fire.' She did. It burned to the ground.

'Oh, bugger,' Murphy advised by phone. 'Well, we'll replace it when it stops raining.'

'What if it dies before he does?' said Mrs Doyle.

'Oh, bugger,' muttered Murphy, who didn't know the answer to that one. Eventually he sold her his first 'Churchill'. She kept it in a warm, dry room awaiting her husband's death.

The job held, people went on dying, most were buried in the 'Powell', which generally held together quite well. Murphy was often heard quietly praying in the funeral parlour's chapel of rest, 'Just don't let it bloody rain!'

Financially he was doing well; his wage was three pounds a week plus a percentage of coffins sold. On a good week he could make fifteen to twenty pounds. He never told

Molly that – she'd have had all of it. Ironically, when the rainy winter months ended, coffin sales declined. The bronchitis season was over and people just refused to die! Murphy's income plummeted.

Money, bloody money. One thing would solve the problem – a robbery. Murphy thought deeply on it and gradually an idea came into his head. Sligo Castle – Lord O'Neill – he'd have money. Now, inside the castle there were suits of armour. If he could get into one and wait for nightfall . . .

Pretending to be the man who read the gas meter, Murphy was allowed entry, despite the fact that the real man who read the gas meter never visited Sligo Castle. They were all-electric. Murphy spotted the suit of armour straight away. There was nobody about. Furtively, he hid all of his clothes in a large chest. Slowly he got into the suit; it was quite comfortable, if cold. He shivered. He sounded like one of those strings of tin cans they tied behind wedding cars. Settling down for a long wait, he tried not to think of the cold. He tried not to think. He was good at that.

Eventually he heard the hall clock strike twelve. The house was silent. Now for action – the safe! Stealthily he crept up the stairs. CLANG! Blast, an arm fell off – no one seemed to have heard. As he walked there was a slight squeaking from the joints. Finally he reached the study. He opened the visor, It slammed shut. He took the helmet off. That was better, now he could see. There on the wall was a picture, behind it, the safe! Now if he could only get the combination right . . . well, he had all night. He proceeded to try various combinations with no luck whatsoever. In the end he tried his old army number, 954042. My God, it worked! The safe opened – there was money inside! He counted it feverishly. It totalled three pounds ten shillings. Surely there must be more? There was, but it was in the Bank of Ireland. Well, so be it. Clutching the money, he put his helmet back on and tiptoed downstairs.

He tried to take the armour off but, curse it, it wouldn't shift. He was still trying to remove it when the early morning butler found him.

'Who are you in there, sir?'

'Mick Murphy,' the armour replied.

'What are you doing in there, Murphy?'

'I'm trying to get out,' said Murphy.

'I'll have to inform the police, sir,' said the butler.

'No, now don't be troublin' yourself by doin' dat. Just help me off wid it and I'll go.'

'No, it's no good, sir, it won't come off. You'll need a plumber,' said the butler, and phoned for one.

Roy Coe, the plumber, assessed the job. It was a tricky one, but it was better than being up to his elbows in shit unblocking some poor diarrhoeic sod's toilet. 'It needs an acetylene torch, but that would burn him to death.'

'Not der torch!' screamed the armour. 'Not der torch!'

Inside, despite the chill of the metal suit, Murphy was pouring with sweat. The plumber decided to cut him out with a hacksaw. First he cut the legs free, revealing Murphy's fat hairy legs.

By now Lord O'Neill was watching. 'Why in God's name, man, did you do this?'

'I was going to a fancy dress ball, sir,' lied Murphy from behind his visor.

By midday, most of the armour was off, but the police had arrived.

'Do you wish to press charges, sir?' asked Garda Michael Milligan, number 213.

The garda were numbered in case they got lost. This was one of the most exciting things ever to have happened in Garda Milligan's short and inauspicious career in law enforcement. Sligo was a dead town. No one was clever enough to be a criminal.

'There's no one to arrest,' he had once complained to his sergeant.

'Oh, dear,' said Garda Sergeant Drew. 'You can always arrest someone for pissing in a doorway.'

Was that true? Milligan had pondered. 'Right, then!' He kept a watchful eye out that night as he was patrolling the street and he caught a couple fornicating in the doorway of a shop.

'And what would youse be doin'?' he asked.

'We're having a shag,' was the answer.

'Is dat so?' nodded Milligan. 'Well, it's a good job youse were not having a piss or I'd have got yer!'

The man in the suit of armour, though, was a different matter altogether. Here was a clear crime in progress. 'So, sir, do you wish to press charges?' repeated Garda Milligan.

'Well, he nicked my elbow wid dat hacksaw, but I'll let him off dis time . . .' said Murphy.

'Not you,' hissed the policeman. 'Your Lordship?'

'Oh, no, officer. I think this is just a joke gone wrong,' he chuckled.

'We can have him for trespass . . .' insisted the policeman.

An hour and a half later, the armour was finally off, revealing Murphy in his vest and underpants, which sent O'Neill into paroxysms of laughter. Sheepishly, Murphy retrieved his clothes from the chest.

'Would sir like a cup of tea?' asked the footman.

Oh, yes, dat was what was needed. Murphy sat drinking it under the watchful eye of the policeman. 'You were lucky to get away wid dis,' he warned.

'Look,' said Murphy, 'I must have bin drunk.'

Garda Milligan eyed Murphy with great suspicion. He knew there was more to Murphy than met the eye, and more would certainly have met the eye had Murphy not kept his underpants on.

Meanwhile, Roy Coe, having dismantled the armour, was having some difficulty in reassembling it. The arms were now welded on backwards and the feet pointed in different directions. Murphy counted himself extremely lucky not to be still inside.

It was one of the few strokes of luck he had ever had. Maybe if he had had a bit more luck, he wouldn't have always been so poor.

'Yes,' thought Murphy, "tis a terrible ting ter be poor . . . a terrible ting ter be poor . . .'

Poverty

Chapter 6

'Yes,' said Murphy, taking a swallow of Guinness as he stood at the bar, ''tis a terrible ting ter be poor.' He said it to Terence Shit.

'It's not as bad as having a name like Shit,' said Terence.

'Ah, but you can change a name like Shit,' said Murphy.

'No, I can't. Me farder wouldn't let me. He wanted me to keep the family name of Shit. He said we came from a long line of Shits. People had kept the Shit name going for centuries; it would be cowardly to change it now.

'He said to me on his deathbed, "If people ask if you are a Shit, don't be afraid to say, 'Yes, I am a Shit!' " '

'Youse will have a hard time gettin' someone to marry you,' said Murphy.

'Yes,' said Terence, 'I suppose I will.'

Terence Shit thought he was fifty-nine. He was a bit out. He was sixty-seven. He had proposed to a hundred and three women without success before becoming engaged to Mary Shane. Even she wasn't sure about marrying him. They had been engaged for twenty-three years.

Terence went to the Post Office to draw his pension. 'I left it as long as I could,' he told the counter clerk.

'Tree months,' said the clerk, counting the money. 'Twelve pounds, six shillins.'

Terence Shit was delighted.

'Oh, I didn't tink it would be so much,' he said, putting it in his pocket. The money went straight through the worn-out pocket, down his leg and out of the ragged bottom of his trouser leg, rolling round the floor. When he picked it all up, it was twelve pounds and *seven* shillings he counted. Somebody else must have dropped a shilling. He wasn't always this lucky.

He threw it down again in the hope it would come up increased. No, it came up as twelve pounds and six shillings. Feck! Still, it was enough to get Mary's engagement ring out of the pawn shop. He'd have to get there before Murphy, though, or the devil would have him back in the bar spending his cash on Guinness all over again.

As it happened, Terence spotted Murphy on the way into the pawn shop and hung back, letting Murphy enter alone. Murphy was a regular visitor to the shop and knew the pawnbroker well. The shop was owned by Hymie Cohen, who swore he wasn't Jewish.

'I've come ter redeem the jockstrap I pawned,' said Murphy, showing Hymie the ticket.

'This ticket is two years old. There will be a lot of interest to pay,' said Hymie, switching on his electronic adding machine. Finally, he said, 'It will be nine pounds five shillings.'

'God almighty, man,' moaned Murphy, 'youse only gave me two shillin' fer it . . . an' me leaving me balls widout der support.'

'Business is business,' said Hymie, waving his hands in the air. 'Look, I'll give you time to pay.'

'How much?'

'How much what? Time or repayment?' asked Hymie. 'Give me ten shillings now and another ten shillings in a week's time. I warn you not to leave the country.'

'But I only earn two pounds a week,' pleaded Murphy. 'You're takin' a tird of it.' His arithmetic had never been that good.

'It's the best I can do,' said Hymie, handing back the jockstrap.

There and then Murphy took off his trousers and started to pull on the jockstrap. At that moment, Mrs Thelma Price, the Lord Mayor's wife, entered. She wanted to pawn a brooch, but stopped in her tracks when she saw Murphy in a state of undress.

'What are you doing, man?' she screamed, seeing the size of Murphy's tackle, twice the size of her husband's.

'Just turn yer back a moment, ma'am,' advised Murphy.

Turn her back on a willy that size? Never! She stood transfixed, fascinated, jealous. Confused, Murphy put both legs in one side of his jockstrap. He hurriedly pulled up his trousers. His balls felt as though they were being strangled. Bent double, he hobbled from the shop, touching his hat to the lady as he left.

Being bent over double, he had no problem seeing the letter from his bank waiting for him on the doormat. Mr Timmins, manager of The Sligo Cooperative Bank wanted to remind him of his overdraft – now outstanding for just over seventeen years – of eight pounds, two shillings and ten pence. Murphy wrote back straight away:

Dear Mr Timmins,
Thank you for writing to me telling me how much my overdraft
is. It was very thoughtful of you. Thank you again.
Yours gratefully
Mick Murphy

That should keep them at bay for another few years. He decided to deliver the letter by hand to save on postage. The bank was on the way to the auction house where Molly had asked him to bid for a gas stove and given him the money. He hoped he hadn't spent too much of it in the pub.

The auctioneer was the aged Mr Cruts. He had asthma which interrupted his attempts to sell anything.

'What-ah-ah-ah-am I bid for this-ah-ah-ah-rolling-ah-ah-ah-pin? Will anyone-ah-ah-ah-say-ah-ah-ah-two pounds?'

'One pound,' said a bidder.

'Any advance on-ah-ah-ah-one pound?' Slamming the mallet down he accidentally smashed a small inkwell. Sotheby's had nothing to fear here.

Came the gas stove, reserve price of five pounds.

'One pound,' said Murphy.

'Two pounds,' called some swine of a man.

'Two pounds and tree pence!' said Murphy.

'Any-ah-ah-ah-advance on-ah-ah-ah-two pounds and three pence?'

'Two pounds and four pence,' said the swine of a man.

So the frenzied bidding continued until Murphy finally outbid him at two pounds and ten pence. Murphy would tell Molly it went for five pounds, the amount she had given him. Less the amount he had already spent in the pub, that left him a clear profit of one pound, three shillings and five pence. With the scent of Guinness already in his nostrils, he dragged the gas stove outside. Now, how to get the bloody thing home? He saw an empty pram parked outside a shop. He heaved the gas stove into it. Thank God, he'd got his jockstrap back. When he wheeled the stove home to Molly, she was delighted. Then came a knock at the door. It was Garda Michael Milligan, number 213.

'What is it dis time, Constable?' asked Murphy.

'You were seen to take a pram from outside a shop in town,' said the policeman.

'Oh, I was just about to put it back,' sighed Murphy.

Accompanied by the policeman, Murphy returned to the store with the pram where a woman, face red with fury, was standing cradling a baby in her arms.

'You bloody tief!' she screamed.

'Sorry, I only borrowed it to take a gas stove home,' explained Murphy.

'A likely story!' she hissed.

'Do you wish to press charges, ma'am?' asked Garda Milligan hopefully.

'Yes I bloody well do!'

Oh, feck.

Murphy was slung in the cells and up before the magistrate the next morning.

In court, the magistrate read the charges. 'You, Michael Murphy, of 210, The Buildings, Sligo, are charged with stealing a pram. Do you plead guilty?' Murphy felt there was an obvious bias towards a guilty verdict in the magistrate's tone.

'I only borrowed it ter take a gas stove home,' said Murphy, sweating profusely.

'Answer the question,' said the magistrate. 'So you plead guilty?'

'Yes, I plead guilty ter borrowing it ter take a gas stove home.'

The magistrate slammed the mallet down and smashed small inkwell. He had no way of knowing that he was secretly the illegitimate stepbrother of Cruts, the auctioneer. 'Fined-ah-ah-ah-ah-ten shillings!'

Find ten shillings? Murphy usually couldn't find *one*. Today he knew he still had one pound three shillings and five pence at hand, but that was so close to being turned into Guinness that it could hardly count.

'Time ter pay, yer honour?' said Murphy.

Yes, the magistrate would give him time to pay. Murphy left the court with his drinking money still intact. Now all he had to do was raise the cash to pay the fine. Outside the court a beggar asked: 'Sor, give us sometin' fer a bite to eat?'

Murphy gave him a pair of false teeth he kept as spares in his pocket.

'God bless you, sor,' said the beggar, fitting the teeth in and biting into a burger.

There was only one way to pay off the fine. He would have to pawn his jockstrap again.

'But you only just redeemed it,' said Hymie. 'How much do you want on it?'

'Der same as der court fine,' said Murphy. 'Ten shillins.'

'I'll give you nine,' said Hymie and Murphy fell for it.

'I've come to pay der fine!' gasped Murphy, rushing back into the court. He slapped nine shillings down on the desk in front of the clerk of the court. 'I'll have ter owe youse der rest.'

Murphy screwed up the receipt and swallowed it. He didn't want any evidence of the underpayment. Now he felt lucky, so the next stop had to be the betting shop in the High Street.

'Dey make a bloody fortune on der likes of us,' he said to another punter, as he slid his money across the counter to the betting shop clerk. 'Two shillins on Lucky Gold in der tree tirty. What's der odds on him?'

'A hundred to one,' said the clerk.

'Oh, dose are good odds,' said Murphy.

'Wid dose odds,' said the clerk, handing Murphy his betting slip, 'he can never win.'

Lucky Gold would have fallen at the first hurdle had he not fallen first in the paddock and been unable to get up again. He was withdrawn from the race.

'Dat's just my bloody luck,' said Murphy. 'But fer dat, he would've won. I should get me money back.'

'No, you don't get yer money back. You nivver do fer a horse dat can't get up,' said the betting clerk.

'I want to see der manager,' said Murphy, and when he saw the manager, immediately regretted the demand. The manager was a huge brute of a man, who slammed his malletlike fist down on the counter, smashing a small inkwell.

'You never get your money back for-ah-ah-ah-ah-a horse that can't get up,' he snarled. 'And-ah-ah-ah-ah-if you want to be able to get up ever-ah-ah-ah-ah-again, you'd better leave now!'

'Have youse many relatives round here?' asked Murphy on his way out the door.

Back in the pub, Murphy nursed his Guinness.

'I wish I could win der Lottery,' he said.

'What would youse do if yer did?' asked the barman.

'First ting I'd shoot der mudder-in-law, den der bank manager, and see what happened.'

'You'd be charged wid murder,' said the barman, farting silently as he did.

'God,' said Murphy. 'Has somebody shit himself? Arrested for murder? I'd plead guilty but insane.'

'You'd be lucky to get away wid it,' said the barman, who was getting away with a smell that filled the pub.

'Somebody has sometin' dead in dem,' said Murphy, realising it was a fart. 'If I did sometin' like dat I would own up to it.' The bloody liar!

Murphy left the pub at his usual time – closing time. It was a cold winter night with driving rain. He would have to get a lift home from someone with a car. The first one he saw passing was Mrs Thelma Price, the Mayor's wife. She wound down the window as she drew up beside him at the kerb.

'Oh, it's yerself, ma'am,' said Murphy. 'I was after a lift home out of dis rain, I don't suppose . . .'

Yes, of course, she could give him a lift. Get in out of the rain quickly. She then took Murphy on the most round-about route home she could imagine, during which with her free hand she tried to agitate his willy. By the time she dropped him off he had an erection like a stallion. He had to wait half an hour outside his own house for it to go down.

'What's fer dinner, darlin'?' he asked, as soon as it was safe to go inside.

He offered no fond greeting to his long-suffering wife, despite the fact that he had been away from home for a whole day, and she expected none. She was just glad to have someone home to eat her latest batch of Irish stew. Molly wasn't really a bad cook, and she wasn't really a bad shag so, after the stew, she gave Murphy a good shag in lieu of pudding. During it he had a fit of sneezing, but it didn't put him off and he kept going. He wasn't bad for a man of his age, although every now and then he had to stop to draw breath.

Murphy spent a great deal of the time out of work and on relief – three shillings a week. Three shillings didn't get much relief. There was always the Sligo Social Centre, though. Murphy and Molly could go there when there was no food in the house and get a free soup and a roll. Sometimes they would get a free handout of potatoes. Was Ireland an endless land of bloody potatoes? During the famine, all the potatoes went rotten, nowadays they were everywhere – in the kitchen, in the loo, in the cellar, everywhere. How did they get in?

With time to kill, Murphy and Molly went to visit the County Fair in a field outside Sligo. They rode on a roundabout. Ah, happy childhood days, he remembered. On reflection, he had never had any happy childhood days. The family was poverty-stricken, his father with the arse out of his trousers and an unemployed alcoholic to boot. His army pension was so small you could hardly see it and his unemployment benefit rarely made it home from the dole office without being converted into Guinness along the way. He had been the perfect role model for Murphy.

On the rifle range, Murphy decided to spend a shilling and test his skill as a marksman: hit the bulls eye and get one of the prizes. 'Yes,' he thought. 'If I win dat teddy bear, I can give it ter Molly. If I win dat bottle of Jameson's, dat's anudder matter.'

The attendant loaded the rifle, Murphy held his breath, aimed at the bull, pulled the trigger, and missed the target completely. Feck.

'I'll get it der next time,' he assured Molly. But no, he didn't get it the next time, nor the next. Finally, he held his breath for his last shot. Bang! Away sped the bullet for a final miss. Feck. He should have brought his reading glasses.

Now he was a shilling down with nothing to show for it. He was determined to recoup his losses. There were other prizes to be won. How far could you pull a lorry with your teeth? A piece of cake! Taking a grip on the rope with his teeth, he pulled and pulled and pulled. His teeth came out. Feck. Never mind, he would pull with his gums. He pulled and pulled and pulled. His gums came out. Feck.

There were other challenges, though.

'Five pounds for anyone who can stay two rounds with Kid Roary!' yelled a man standing in a makeshift boxing ring.

'Five pounds!' thought Murphy 'Dat's a fortune! An' all fer a couple of rounds of der boxin' wid some kid. I'm fer dat.'

Murphy sat in his corner waiting for the bell. Opposite him was a slightly built but mean-looking young boxer. Clang-clang! Murphy rose at the bell to face up to Kid Roary. He came to to hear the referee say, ' . . . nine, ten, out!'

'Dat's unfair!' said Murphy. 'He hit me when me eyes was closed.'

'Yes,' said the referee, 'he closed them for you.'

For his brief survival, he was awarded five shillings. It was better than nothing, but only just.

Next he spotted the hammer test. You hit the button to see how far the arrow went up, the aim being to ring the bell at the top. Taking hold of the hammer, he whirled it above his head and brought it down with great force on his boot.

'Ow! Jesus!' he screamed, as he hopped around clutching his foot.

What next? Next he paid for using the hammer. 'Pay? But I missed,' he moaned.

'Youse didn't miss, man,' said the fairground attendant. 'Youse made a perfect hit on yer boot.'

Ah! A gypsy. She would tell his fortune. She did. It came to three shillings. A desire was deep in him to try the rifle range again.

'Dis time I won't miss,' he promised himself. 'Sure an' me farder shot der Kaiser, didn't he? He was always tellin' me so. He came home from der war an' said "I shot der Kaiser." If me farder can shoot der Kaiser, I can shoot der bull.'

He took careful aim at the target, squeezed the trigger and hit the attendant.

'I'm sorry,' Murphy apologised. 'I was aimin' fer der Kaiser.'

Fancy having to pay to shoot the attendant. He wished now that he had shot the Kaiser. He'd now spent everything he had, including the money he'd won by being laid out by Kid Roary. He'd teach these capitalists. He'd use the free toilet and use lots and lots of arse paper. He'd even take some home with him. It would be on his conscience, but on Saturday he could confess it to Father Brenan.

Come Saturday, the priest forgave Murphy and told him not to go stealing any more arse paper. After that Murphy felt free, free to use as much of his stolen arse paper as he liked. Just his luck. He was constipated. It got so bad that he hadn't been for fourteen days, or if he had, he didn't remember it. Fancy having a shit and not remembering it. No, that couldn't be right. He'd gone for fourteen days without.

'Now dat,' reckoned Murphy, 'should be in der *Guinness Book of Records*.'

He phoned and told them, but they said it wasn't a record. They didn't encourage record breaking of that sort, but if they did, it was certain to be more than twice Murphy's fourteen days. Aha! So if Murphy just hung on a little longer he could break the record.

By the eighteenth day he was becoming seriously ill and the district nurse had to give him an enema.

'I suppose you know you're ruining me chances of getting in ter der *Guinness Book of Records*,' he said.

Once he was back on his feet again, Murphy went for a stroll around town. After all that activity in his bowels, he felt hungry. He was passing the YMCA, so popped in and asked, 'Can youse oblige me wid der loan of a cheese sandwich?'

Yes, they could, thank feck! Murphy took his cheese sandwich to a restaurant to eat. It seemed the right place to go to eat. He seated himself at a table and the waiter approached, wanting to know if he wanted to order anything.

'No,' said Murphy. 'I'm already eatin', but can I 'ave a sample cup of tea?'

The answer was yes, but he couldn't drink it there or he would have to pay for it, so he took it outside to drink and left the cup on the pavement. God, what a terrible thing it was to be without money. The sandwich had cured his hunger, although he supposed he could have sold it.

He made his way home where Molly was waiting.

'Where have youse been? Yer bloody dinner is gettin' cold.'

It was Irish stew – what else? He had hoped that the cheese sandwich would have curbed his hunger to the extent that he wouldn't feel the need to eat any of Molly's latest mess of Irish stew. Irish stew, Irish stew, Irish stew, seven days a bloody week. Hadn't she ever heard of Chicken Marengo? No, she hadn't. Feck. Neither had he.

'Youse are really needin' a new suit,' said Molly, duti-fully mending the seat of Murphy's trousers for the tenth time.

No he didn't. It was good for another ten years at least. He changed his mind when kneeling at Mass and his balls dropped through his trousers. Keeping his legs together, he went home early from Mass, to the surprise of his wife. Molly never really expected Murphy home till after closing time

'Oh, darlin', youse was right,' he said. 'I need a new suit. Me balls has dropped tru me trousers.'

'Mullins is der man ter make youse a suit,' advised Molly. 'He'll give us it on der nivver nivver.'

Sean Mullins, the tailor, measured Murphy for his new suit. 'Yes,' he said, 'I'll have dis suit ready in tree weeks.'

But Mullins got himself all mixed up. Measures used to be in feet and inches, but now they had gone metric. Metres and centimetres. The result? The jacket was enormous but the trousers came to just below the knee.

'I'm not payin' fer dis!' howled Murphy from somewhere inside the jacket.

'I'm sorry, Murphy,' said Mullins. 'I'll try again.'

'Not on me, you don't,' said Murphy, escaping through one of the sleeves.

Molly would just have to work miracles with his trousers one more time. He certainly wasn't wearing Mullins' ridiculous effort – trousers halfway up his legs. Halfway up his legs? That reminded him – the Masons! He had been a Mason for seven years. Yes, they would help him in hard times . . . and that time was now! The mother lodge was in Scotland. He wrote straight away:

Dear Brother
I have been a brother for seventy years. I am now a hundred
years old and very short of money. Can you help, please?
Brother Michael Murphy
Grand Master
1959

They wrote back enclosing a cheque for a pound.

'Mean bastards!' cried Murphy. 'One bloody pound! And wid der balls hangin' out of me trousers.'

Saint Patrick. He was Murphy's patron saint. He would pray to him for money. At Mass Murphy prayed so hard he had to sit down. The collection was handed round and offered to the priest who addressed the congregation.

'God help youse all,' he said. 'By the number of buttons in the plate it's a wonder your clothes aren't falling off you. The Mass is ended. Go in peace.'

Murphy cringed. He had taken a two shilling piece from the plate. God would strike him dead. He waited, he didn't.

'Oh, dat was a close ting,' he said, crossing himself.

On the way home, he decided to make the best use of whatever talents he had in order to make a living, or at least the price of a pint. He threw his hat on the pavement in front of him and started to sing.

Oh, Rose Marie, I love youse
I'm always tinkin' of youse
I bless der way and bless der day
I met youse . . .

He couldn't remember any more, so he started again.

THE MURPHY

Oh, Rose Marie, I love youse
I'm always tinkin' of youse . . .

'Stop!' said a man. 'Are you trying to earn money?'
'Yes, dat's der idea.'
'Man, with that voice, you'll never see any!'
Never one to give in easily, Murphy went on singing for an hour. The man was right. Not a penny appeared. Perhaps dat feller was right, thought Murphy. Der general public maybe doesn't appreciate a voice like mine. I needs an instrument. Der spoons! Dat's it, I'll play der spoons!

He borrowed two spoons from a restaurant, the waiter agreeing to lend him them on the understanding that he wouldn't leave them on the pavement like he did with the cup of tea, and that he could have them back in time for dessert.

Murphy soon had the spoons clickety-clacking, but, before he was warmed up enough to attract any sort of donation in his hat, he was interrupted by the waiter. 'I'm sorry, we need to have them back, someone's ordered pudding already.'

Feck. Life was hell. You couldn't earn any bloody money. Murphy ambled back home.

'Youse look tired, Mick,' said Molly.
'Yes, I bin playin' der spoons,' he said.
'What was yer playin' on der spoons?'
'I was playin' Beethoven's Fifth Symphony.'
'Dat must have been hard on der spoons,' commented Molly.
'No, really, it all came back to me,' he said.
Of course, he hadn't been playing Beethoven's Fifth Symphony. He was playing Rachmaninov's Second Piano

Concerto, but he wasn't going to tell *her* that. Playing Rachmaninov's Second Piano Concerto was easy on the spoons. You just had to remember where you were. Once you remembered that, the rest was easy. Murphy remembered he was in Sligo High Street. After that it was a piece of cake.

If only everything in life was that simple, but things always managed to become so complicated.

'Bein' married,' mumbled Murphy, 'and der sex ting. Now dem's nivver der most simplest tings in der world, is dey . . ?'

*Love &
Marriage*

Chapter 7

Away on the edge of Sligo, dancing at the Dreamland Ballroom, was a lass called Molly Yates. A young, gawky lad had asked her to dance. She was wishing he hadn't. He had crashed her into couple after dancing couple.

'Sure, you're a lovely dancer,' he grinned, crashing her into the building supports.

'Dat's enough,' she said.

'I'll show youse to yer seat,' he grinned.

'No, thanks, I know the way.' Sure enough, she knew the way.

Eyeing her from the other side of the room was local football hero Eric McQuade: tall, good-looking and well built, but an idiot.

'Can I have der next waltz wid you?' he asked

The next dance was a quick step. Never mind, he would waltz to it, anyway.

'*One*, two, *tree*,' he whispered to her, as they took to the floor.

'No, no,' she said. 'It's one, two, three, *four*.'

'Oh, I was one short,' he said, but went on *one*, two, *three*. The band stopped but Eric McQuade went on waltzing.

'Der band has stopped,' said Molly.

'Oh, I don't need a band. All I needs is you,' he beamed.

95

'Please let me go,' she said, and, after a pause, 'I nivver want ter see youse again.'

She didn't appreciate good dancin', thought McQuade, Nivver wants ter see me again, is it? She must be mad. Doesn't she know I scored two goals against Shabeen United? And is that der dirty devil Murphy sneakin' up on her dere? I tort I saw him after her earlier . . .

Indeed he had. Murphy had crashed around the dance floor with Molly just before McQuade had taken over. To Molly he certainly seemed more likeable than the bampot McQuade and, although he had no real sense of style, there was something about this Murphy . . .

Molly was a vegetarian. 'Oh, den you only eats bran,' said Murphy.

No, she didn't only eat bran, she ate vegetables. 'And youse is a bloody meat eater – disgusting,' she said. 'You like lamb chops? Did youse know dat dey slaughter two million lambs a year?'

'Oh, Molly, I only eat one of dem. I'm really an Irish vegetarian. I only eats animals dat eats grass. Hee-hee.'

'To tink of dem poor suffering farm animals, crammed together in lorries, den on to cattle ships, den to der abattoirs, and . . .'

'I don't kill dem,' said Murphy.

'Yes, but dey are killin' dem for *you*,' said Molly.

'I don't ask dem to,' he protested. 'All I do is eat dem when dey are dead, and eating dem den, dey don't feel a ting.'

Here was a man, thought Molly, who stuck to his guns, but they weren't loaded.

In years to come she would always remind him of their wedding anniversary on 5 October. Murphy didn't need reminding, he would never forget. He was at the altar with Molly with a heavy cold, sneezing throughout the whole ceremony. Because of that, a ceremony that should have been over in twenty minutes lasted an hour and a quarter.

For the honeymoon he had booked them in at a posh hotel in Dublin, the Hibernian.

'Ah, welcome, sor, and congratulations,' said a loud-voiced porter as they arrived.

'Could youse serve us porridge for two in our room at nine tirty,' asked Murphy.

By midnight they had fecked themselves half to death. Next morning on the dot of nine thirty there was a knock at the door.

'Who is it?' groaned Murphy.

'It's der porridge,' came the reply.

They ate it sitting up in bed. After that they were at it again until they fell sleep. Eventually, they made it down to the restaurant. They looked at the menu. It was in French.

'Look, Molly,' said Murphy, 'I don't understand any of dis. I'll order eggs and chips.'

The waiter who took the order was in shock. 'Er . . . any special wine, sir?'

'Yes,' said Murphy. 'Any special wine.'

After their eggs and chips they strolled to the museum to see the *Book of Kells*. Both it and the museum were closed.

'What is der *Book of Kells*?' asked Molly.

'It's a book of colours done by der monks a long time ago.'

'I suppose dey will all be dead now?' said Molly.

'I hope so,' said Murphy. 'If dey're not, dey must be tree hundred years old.'

They made for the National Gallery. There was a portrait of the big feller, Michael Collins.

'He was a fine man, Molly,' said Murphy. 'He led der IRA during der troubles.'

'What troubles?' asked Molly.

'Der civil war, Molly,' explained Murphy. 'It was terrible: brudder shooting brudder. And on top of dat, der English shot Kevin Barry.'

'Had he done sometin' wrong?'

'He shot some English bastard in the balls,' said Murphy.

'He must have been aimin' a bit low,' was Molly's comment.

'Look, I'm tired of walking now,' said Murphy. 'Let's go back and have a shag.'

'Oh, Mick, you're so romantic.'

So they went back to the hotel and had a shag, then two or three more. In between, Murphy read the *Irish Times*. There was an article about the discovery of Tutankhamen's tomb.

'Did dey just dig him up?' asked Molly.

'Yes, I suppose so.'

'What's der point of diggin' up a stiff?' she said.

Murphy didn't know, but it was obviously an important stiff.

'I tink dat when dey bury a person dey should leave dem dere,' said Molly.

'Dey usually do,' nodded Murphy. 'When I die I want ter be left dere.'

'Do youse ever tink if dyin'?'

'Oh, yes,' said Murphy, 'but I don't do it.'

'A time will come when yer do,' she said.

'Yes, but dat's not yet.'

It was time for another honeymoon feck, so they went ahead and had one.

'You're a good shag, Molly,' Murphy complimented her.

'Tank you, Mick. Dat's nice ter know.'

To think she had thought of becoming a nun. She was not a great loss to the order.

They had a good life together. Molly was a good wife to Murphy and they had two children, Silé and Sean. Sean had joined the British Army where the pay was better than the Irish. He had joined the Irish Guards, being six foot tall.

On guard outside Buckingham Palace at two in the morning on a foggy night, young Sean Murphy couldn't see his hand in front of his face. It wasn't there. Had it been there, he would have been on a charge for not standing to attention properly. In any case, the fog was so thick that, had he been permitted to put his hand in front of his face, he wouldn't have been able to see it. Consequently, at the least noise he would spring into the alert position. If he had said, 'Halt! Who goes dere, friend or foe?' once, he had said it a hundred bloody times. God, he was grateful when his relief arrived, although he challenged him, too.

'Halt! Who goes dere, friend or foe?'

'Friend, yer silly bugger,' was the answer.

Sean needed a compass to find his way back to the barracks. After a while he realised that he was in the middle of Piccadilly, clearly heading in totally the wrong direction. He had to get a taxi back to the barracks.

'Where the bloody hell have you been, Murphy?' roared the Duty Sergeant.

Murphy explained, to the uncontrolled laughter of his companions. 'Piccadilly Circus?' said one. 'You could've picked up a good shag dere!'

Why, oh why, had he joined the Irish bloody Guards? Yes, there was the better pay. Yes, he wanted to get away from the girl he had put in the pudden club. Yes, he needed to escape from his nagging bloody mother. Well, they were all pretty good reasons, but was it really worth it? All those hours square bashing. 'Look to yer bloody front, soldier! Stand still you 'orrible little man!' The insults were endless and he was stuck with it. He couldn't even go home on leave to Sligo; that girl's father would kill him. He was forever trapped in bloody England.

His commanding officer was Major Harold Alexander. He was a brave officer with an MC and DSO. He was brave, but stupid. Young Murphy reckoned you had to be stupid to be brave. Life-or-death heroics weren't clever, they were stupid, but then so was Murphy. He was fully qualified to become the bravest soldier ever. No, guardsman Murphy wasn't very intelligent, but in the Guards that really wasn't very important. Murphy had been told their job was 'to do or die'. So far he had done the 'do' part but had as yet to do the 'die' part.

Some of guardsman Murphy's wages were sent home to Sligo. The contribution was welcomed by his family. It helped with food bills and to pay his father's drink bills. His father was eternally grateful for that.

Life without Guinness was unthinkable for Murphy, so Murphy didn't think it. Instead, thinking of his child far away in the Irish Guards made him reminisce about his own childhood. It had been a turbulent upbringing with a crippled, drunken father.

Mind you, thought Murphy, he wasn't always a crippled drunk. Dat was me mudder's doin'. She crippled him ter get der sick benefit. She waited till he was asleep den hit his legs wid a hammer. He didn't feel a ting until he woke up in der mornin', but by den it was too late; by den he was a cripple.

Sure an' he was a good crippled farder, though. He brought tings home fer us. A policeman's truncheon once. Der policeman came ter der house and took it back der next day. One night he brought home a farm horse. It shit all over der floor. Next day he had to take it back, but by den we were knee deep in horse shit. We spent all day shovellin' der bloody stuff out. Dat was hard work . . .'

Hard work was something always to be avoided. Murphy quite often found himself drawing the dole. It wasn't much, but it kept the wolf from the door. 'Why do people say dat? A wolf has nivver ivver come to our door.'

Molly was a good housekeeper. Mind you, it wasn't a very good house, more like a shack. She was a good shack keeper, and an economical shopper – two penneth of this and two penneth of that. That's what he had to eat, two penneth of this and two penneth of that.

'Don't leave anyting,' Molly would say at mealtimes. There was never anyting to bloody leave. In the summer he would read the *Irish Times* in the park and maybe he'd feed the pigeons if he had enough bread left over from breakfast. So he rarely fed them. Then near lunch time he'd go to the pub for bread and cheese. He took his own bread and had the pub's cheese, that and a Guinness, which he took two hours to drink.

'Are youse havin' trouble wid dat?' said der barman.

'I likes ter take me time,' he said.

'Well mind yer don't run out of time,' said the barman. 'We close in nine hours.'

From the pub he would go to the Public Library, with its store of 80 books.

'Is dat book on der Virgin Birth back yet?'

No, it wasn't. Would he like an alternative book?

'Yes, *Der Fall of Der Roman Empire*,' he said. The librarian sighed over the waste of ink and stamped his card.

Murphy took the book home.

'What in God's name have you got dere?' said Molly, gawking at the huge volume.

'It's *Der Fall of Der Roman Empire.*'

'What in God's name are you readin' dat for?'

'Because der Virgin Birth book is still out.'

That completely flummoxed her. It was the first time in her life she had been flummoxed and she didn't like it. The huge book took up half the table.

'Dere isn't any room ter serve der dinner!' So she served it on *The Fall of The Roman Empire*. Murphy had to eat it before he could start reading the book. Once he started, he couldn't put it down, only to rest his arms. He took it to bed, was it tired? He was fascinated by the Coliseum.

'Jesus, how terrible, dem sending dose Christians to der lions. Why didn't der Pope stop dem? Dat was very lax of him. What did Christians taste like? Dey must have tasted nice or der lions wouldn't eat dem.'

He fell asleep dreaming of gladiators and at breakfast he told Molly all about them.

'Those gladiators fort each udder ter death!' he said.

'Silly buggers, dem,' said Molly.

'Have youse no romance in yer soul, woman?' he said.

'When yer cookin' and cleanin' twenty-four hours a day, dere's little room fer bloody romance!' she scowled.

Yes, that sounded reasonable. He'd noticed the romance seeping out of their relationship the previous summer when he had been hiring out deck chairs and donkeys on the beach. A penny for a deck chair, tuppence for a donkey ride. A mother wanted to give her kid a donkey ride.

'Dat'll be tuppence, ma'am.'

The mother wanted to ride behind.

'Madam. Wid your weight, it would break der poor animal's back.'

So the kid rides alone, the donkey unseats the kid and the mother wants her money back. Murphy offers her a penny and she whacks him round the head with her handbag.

She must have had an anchor in it. Murphy saw stars and nursed the bruise on the back of his head as he handed over the tuppence.

That wasn't as bad as the clout he'd received from one of his deck chair clients. He had set out all the deck chairs one morning when he noticed the tide starting to come in. By the time he had helped everyone to move further up the beach, water was lapping around people's feet and some of them wanted their money back. Murphy decided to do a runner. One man with a deck chair did a faster runner and smacked him round the head with it. Feck.

In a fortnight he made five pounds. Astounding! Paying for the donkey hire left him with thirteen shillings. Feck.

'Tirteen shillin's will buy me tree Guinnesses,' figured Murphy, 'leavin' ten shillins fer Molly.'

'Ten bloody shillins after two week's work?' howled Molly. 'What am I supposed ter do wid dat?'

'Spend it,' he advised, dodging a right to the jaw, only to go down to a left to the jaw. The back of his head hit the floor and there he remained.

'How long are youse goin' ter lay dere, man?' yelled Molly.

'Till I come to,' he said.

Well, while he was down he might as well have a little sleep.

He woke up next morning with the Hoover running over him.

'Fer God's sake, woman, can't youse tell der difference between me and der carpet?' he fumed, tenderly touching the lump on the back of his head.

'I tried ter go over you as quietly as I could,' she said.

'God knows why I married you,' he said.

'Because I'm a good shag,' she replied. So saying, she felt in her handbag for her dill-doll to assure herself.

A good shag? thought Murphy. Once upon a time, maybe.

He recalled their last shag. It was twelve years ago. He dimly remembered it had been a success, though he had lost a stone doing it. He must nivver lose that much weight again. The shag had lasted two hours. During the second hour, she fell asleep, but that didn't stop him. Once he started something he always finished it. During the last ten minutes he woke her up so she could join in the fun.

He recalled his own last shag. Having managed to accumulate a modest amount of cash, he had decided to try out the night life in Dublin. Scratz Disco. One of those new-fangled disco dance-hall things. He walked downstairs to mind-thumping rock music. He looked more than a little out of place in his funeral suit, collar and tie. Half of the dancers were half-naked. There was a girl on her own. No, she didn't dance with men, she was a lesbian. Could he sit and talk to her?

'OK, what's an old creep like you doin' in here?'

'I'm tryin' ter improve der quality of me life,' explained Murphy.

'Haven't you left it a bit late?'

'Steady on, woman, I'm only fifty-six.'

'God, man. You're nearly dead.'

'Would you like a foxtrot?'

'What in God's name is dat?'

Murphy explained that it was a dance. She explained that he could do it on his own. So he got on the dance floor and did a foxtrot on his own – everyone stopped to watch. He left the disco to the laughter of the crowd.

The girl followed him and asked him if he'd like a shag to make him feel better. They did it there and then in the alleyway and it did make him feel better. Would she like him to take her to dinner? She would love it. They stood in the drizzle eating fish and chips from the *Irish Times*. Yes, the night life in Dublin wasn't too bad at all.

'Where in God's name have you been, man?' came the familiar greeting when he got home.

'I've been doin' der foxtrot.'

'Who wid?'

'Meself.'

'Yerself. Yer a fool.'

'No one else could do it.'

'Mrs Riley can foxtrot.'

'Mrs Riley wasn't dere, Molly.'

'What's der use of talking ter dis silly bugger?'

'Damn and blast you, woman, I am not a silly bugger!'

'Earnie Woods is a silly bugger.'

'Sure an' dat's true enough,' admitted Murphy. 'Earnie Woods is as daft as a trumpet.' The mere mention of the madman's name had made the old wound on the back of his head start to throb.

'He's happy enough in der lunatic asylum, though,' said Molly. 'I heard today dat he has tree meals a day which he trows at der cook. Der priest visits him twice a week and Earnie empties der piss-pot over him.'

'He's not completely mad, den,' mused Murphy. He remembered the rock hitting the back of his head with a clang. With a clang? Rocks didn't go clang, did they? A frying pan, now that went clang when it hit you. He could certainly hear that clang – and feel it. Ouch! Jesus, there it was again . . .

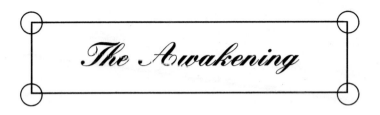

Chapter 8

She stood over him with the frying pan raised, ready to give him another whack.

'Oh, Molly, I know I've been a bad husband to you . . .'

'Youse have just said dat,' she frowned, 'an' youse were right both times.'

'Molly, darlin', I'll make it up to you.'

'Youse have just said dat, too.'

'I did?'

'Yes, Dad, you did.' It was Silé. Of course, she came in halfway through the little discussion he and Molly were having, but she could only have been standing there for a few seconds. Had he really gone back over all that old ground in less time than it takes to pour a Guinness? He spotted a small movement out of the corner of his eye and turned to see Molly drawing back for another swing.

'No, Molly,' he pleaded. 'Stop wid der whacks on der head. I tink I'm taking bad wid it.'

'Dat's der whole idea,' said Molly.

'No, no!' he held up his hands in surrender and heaved himself out of bed. 'Look how I'm up and on me feet an' everytin'.'

He held his head in his hands, dizzy with the sudden effort. Had he really been such a drunken useless bugger all his life? Why had Molly put up with him all these years? 'But fer us being Catholics, I'd have divorced you bloody years ago.' Yes, he remembered her saying that now. Feck.

'Tings is goin' ter change, Molly,' he promised. 'I'm goin' ter make tings better for you. Yer a good woman. Youse deserve a husband you can rely on.'

'Dat's true,' Molly agreed. 'If youse find one when yer at work, send him here wid yer wages.'

'No, Molly,' said, Murphy, straightening his back and standing tall. 'I'm goin' ter be dat husband yer can rely on. I'm goin' ter give up der drinkin'. I'm goin' ter work hard fer youse. I'm goin' back ter der buildin' site now. I'll be home at tea time wid me wages.'

Determined to be true to his word, Murphy hurried to the site and worked harder than he had ever done before, including two hours in the rain for the extra three pence an hour. When he picked up his wage packet at the end of the day, for once he really felt he had earned it. He smiled proudly to himself as he strode off the site with the rest of the men, their boots heavy with mud and clumping on the cobbles.

'Aren't youse comin' fer a jar, Murphy?' came a voice.

Suddenly, Murphy realised that he was two paces ahead of the others, who had all stopped by the door of the pub.

'Not me,' said Murphy, 'I'm . . .'

Mind you. He had worked in the rain for the extra pay, hadn't he? And half an hour in the pub, wouldn't make much difference, would it? And the odd pint now and again wouldn't hurt, would it?

THE MURPHY

'Well, just a quick one, den,' he said and, with the scent of Guinness in his nostrils overpowering the pang of broken promises, Murphy drifted into the pub . . .

Other books by

SPIKE MILLIGAN . . .

A MAD MEDLEY OF MILLIGAN

Said Prince Charles
When they placed
The Crown on his head
I suppose this means
That Mummy's dead

A wonderful collection of new poems, jokes, doodles, giggles and general hilarity – including the historical epic 'Adolf Hitler, Dictator and Clown'.

First published 1999

ISBN 1 85227 845 5   £8.99 hb

SPIKE MILLIGAN

A Celebration

The Best of Milligan

With cringeworthy grovelling from Eric Sykes, Sir Harry Secombe, Denis Norden, Ronnie Scott, Jim Dale, Mrs Gladys Scroake, etc . . .

A cornucopia of classic Milliganese, *Spike Milligan: A Celebration* includes some of Spike's funniest material, and is illustrated throughout with a unique collection of photographs.

As well as poetry and short stories, this book features two complete *Goon Show* scripts, along with an excerpt from a third; scenes from the play *The Bedsitting Room* and the complete script for the film *The Case of the Mukkinese Battlehorn*.

There are specially selected excerpts from Spike's hilarious war memoirs and his novels *Puckoon* and *The Looney*, sketches from his *Q* television series and examples of his prolific output as a compaigning letter writer.

Scattered throughout the book are tributes and reminiscences from some of those who have known and worked with Spike over the years, making this a true celebration of a great comic talent.

*No 1 bestseller in Ireland
*Top 10 UK bestseller
**Daily Mail* 'Top Five Read'

First published 1995

ISBN 1 85227 561 8   £9.99 hb
ISBN 0 86369 929 4   £6.99 pb

THE GOONS – THE STORY

Edited by Norma Farnes

The Goons first came together in a pub called The Grafton Arms in London's Victoria, where landlord Jimmy Grafton created a haven for up-and-coming actors, comics and writers in the early post-war years, serving up advice and encouragement along with the beer. Spike Milligan was renting a room above the pub and working on scripts with Grafton when his wartime friend, Harry Secombe, introduced him to Peter Sellers and Michael Bentine.

There then began a terrible, rasping, squealing, giggling, snorting period of lunacy, which continued unabated until 1960. The Goons first went on air at the BBC as *The Crazy People* on 28 May 1951. It wasn't until the second series in 1952 that the BBC agreed to change the name of the show to *The Goon Show*. Spike, of course, became the driving force behind the Goons, writing the scripts and devising the characters which became part of our comic heritage.

There remains a huge interest in the Goons, with each new generation (mainly thanks to tapes and CDs) discovering afresh the anarchic humour which has had such a massive influence on so many of our top comedy performers.

Norma Farnes, Spike's manager since 1965, has overseen the compilation of this unique collection of Spike's personal memorabilia and photographs. With contributions from Sir Harry Secombe and Eric Sykes (co-writer of some two dozen *Goon Shows*) and a select band of Goons *aficionados*, this book forms a fascinating history of an enduring comic phenomenon.

First published 1997

ISBN 1 85227 679 7 £16.99 hb

BLACK BEAUTY

According to Spike Milligan

The legend of Black Beauty has spawned (if a horse can be said to spawn; it's more of a froggy thing, really) a great may horsey tales on film, television and in print, but even Anna Sewell's original classic adventure failed to tell it like it really is.

Here, straight from the horse's mouth, is *Black Beauty According to Spike Milligan*, revealing what it's like to be a young foal:

> As soon as I was old enough to eat grass, my mother used to stuff it down my throat until it kept coming out the back.

Or to be sold be a beloved master:

> I could not say goodbye, so I put my nose in his hand and bit off a finger.

Or to be out in freezing cold weather:

> The horses all felt it very much. I felt mine and it was frosty.

Spike canters through this volume in his bestselling *According to . . .* series with a bawdy irreverence, and adds a unique element by introducing each chapter with a new poem.

As befits a tale of earthy, horsey folk, earthy, horsey, strong language is used.

First published in 1996

ISBN 1 85227 615 0   £9.99 hb
ISBN 0 7535 0102 3   £4.99 pb

FRANKENSTEIN

According to Spike Milligan

Mary Shelley's Frankenstein was a sorely troubled man, haunted by his conscience over the creature he had created.

Spike Milligan's Frankenstein is equally haunted – haunted by the image of his poorly stitched together creation in his poorly stitched together trousers (will they never stay up?) roaming the countryside with it hanging out, terrifying the populace, scrounging fags and desperate for a shag.

Just like Mary Shelley's original story of *Frankenstein*, Spike's version is a tale of brooding torment. The fact that Spike has built plenty of laughs into the brooding torment just goes to show where the Shelley woman went wrong.

Mary Shelley's characters may never have used the kind of strong language uttered by Spike's versions, but I bet they often wanted to.

First published in 1997

ISBN 1 85227 609 6   £9.99 hb
ISBN 0 7535 0227 5   £4.99 pb

ROBIN HOOD

According to Spike Milligan

Sharper than the edge of a mighty broadsword and slicker than a speeding arrow, Spike rampages through the tale of *Robin Hood* like an outlaw on the run through Sherwood Forest.

All of Robin's merry men are in attendance in Spike's *Robin Hood*, although not quite as they were in the original version. Maid Marian is a champion pole-vaulter, Little John has been renamed Big Dick (for reasons we need not go into here) and Will Scarlet and Friar Tuck are joined by a brand new addition to the renegade band – Groucho Marx.

Together the men, and women, of Sherwood do battle against the evil Prince John, the despicable Sheriff of Nottingham and the loathsome Sir Guy de Custard Gisborne.

'Who loosed that arrow?' demanded Prince John.

He turned as he spoke and saw a man wearing a green cloak over his suit of brown widdling against a tree.

'Who goes there?' called the Prince, pointing to the tree.

'We all do.'

You've never seen anything like this in green tights before.

First published 1998

ISBN 1 85227 732 7   £10.99 hb
ISBN 0 7535 0303 4   £4.99 pb

TREASURE ISLAND

According to Spike Milligan

This is the final volume of Spike's hilarious reinterpretations of classic works of literature. All of the familiar faces from Robert Louis Stevenson's original version join in the fun – Squire Trelawney, Jim Hawkins and Long John Silver, but they are joined, as were the men of Sherwood in Spike's *Robin Hood*, by Groucho Marx.

Long John's parrot plays a starring role:

> And the parrot would say with great rapidity, 'Pieces of eight! Pieces of eight!' til you wondered that it was not out of breath, or til John threw his handkerchief over the cage. 'Take that bloody cloth off my cage!' screamed the parrot.

The rip-roaring adventure of the hunt for buried treasure unravels faster than Ben Gunn's pants, with plenty of laughs along the way. Even the sad bits are funny:

> Hunter never regained consciousness. He lingered all day and died, so I ate his dinner.

Rude and irreverent as ever, Spike's rendering of this classic tale is as chock full of gems as Cap'n Flint's treasure chest.

Robert Louis Stevenson will probably never know how Spike rewrote his story, but then he probably never knew that his name was an anagram of 'bonniest love trousers' either.

First published 2000

ISBN 1 85227 895 1   £10.99 hb

SPIKE MILLIGAN – THE FAMILY ALBUM

An Illustrated Autobiography

For years Spike Milligan has lovingly collected and collated over a dozen precious volumes of family photographs and memorabilia, stretching from Army life in India in 1869, his birth in 1918 and his childhood, to his life as an entertainer and the arrival of his own family. Spike has carefully selected scores of these very personal photographs to illustrate his intriguing family history and the story of his career, creating a fascinating record of his amazing life.

In writing *The Family Album*, Spike has overcome a major personal hurdle. At times touching and deeply intimate, this book includes details of how Spike was plagued by manic depression stemming from his wartime experiences. His subsequent traumatic mental breakdown and the collapse of his first marriage led him to believe that he could never bring himself to write an autobiography such as this. *The Family Album* is an inspiring, poignant retrospective from a true comic genius.

First published 1999

ISBN 1 85227 886 2   £20.00 hb